THE LINEAGE OF
LOVE

SHYAH DICKERSON

LITTLE ENGINE ∞ PROJECT

The Lineage of Love copyright © 2022 Shyah Dickerson.

All rights reserved.

Printed in the United States of America. No part of this book may be used or reproduced in any manner without written permission except in the case of brief quotations embodied in critical articles and reviews.

For information, address Little Engine Project, P.O. Box 115272 Atlanta, Georgia 30310

Library of Congress Cataloging-in-Publication available
Printed in the United States of America

Book design by Lauren Johnson/Providence & Design, LLC
Edited by Pathway Coach Writing

ISBN: 978-1-7376837-7-6

I dedicate this book to the memory of my Grandmothers', because of you, I am.

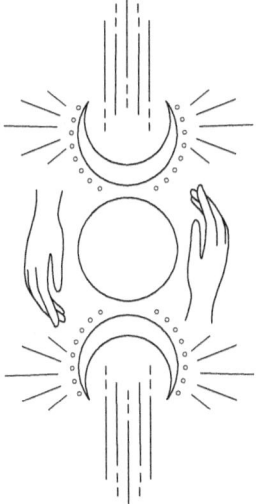

I dedicate this book to the memory

of my Grandmothers', because of

you, I am.

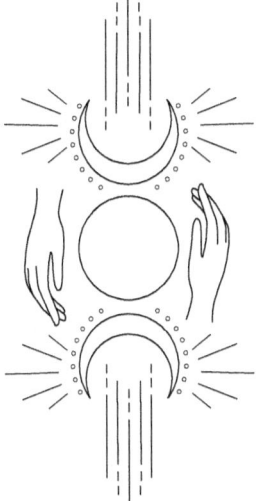

CONTENTS

intro:	ẹ káàbọ̀	1

PART I

chapter 1	the way	11
chapter 2	coming into being	18
chapter 3	power source	28
chapter 4	substance of things hoped for	33
chapter 5	religious pursuits	39
chapter 6	evidence of things not seen	47

PART II

chapter 7	keys to the kingdom	57
chapter 8	liberating your desire	65
chapter 9	choice	70
chapter 10	healing dis-ease	77
chapter 11	integrity	85
chapter 12	soul ties	90
chapter 13	commitment	99

PART III

chapter 14	golden journey	109
chapter 15	portal of initiation	115
chapter 16	your edge	122
chapter 17	take up your crown	127
chapter 18	otito	133
outro:	modupe	139
index		143

Ẹ KÁÀBỌ
WELCOME

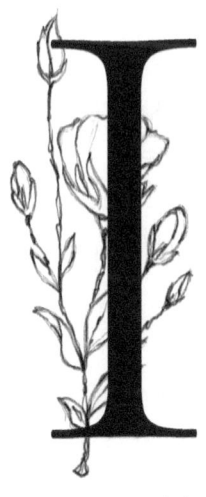

I was alone in my apartment in excruciating pain from undiagnosed Lyme Disease. Early one morning, just hours before sunrise, I screamed into my pillow, tears streaming down my face,

"God, please help me!" This particular morning, I was wearier than I ever remembered. This felt like an end, and I earnestly needed God to step in and help me. For the entirety of my life, I have had a very intimate and burgeoning relationship with *Spirit*. Our relationship had been through many spaces. This current space required growth and expansion. I was deepening spiritually, and it was deathly uncomfortable.

Moving from my hometown New York City to Atlanta had catapulted me into the unknown. My survival tactics were proving to be insufficient. That dark morning when I was screaming in my pillow, I reached a pivotal moment in my journey. I could continue to yell into the pillow for God, or I could surrender and listen to the messages this pain was petitioning to reveal. Teary-eyed and afraid, I chose to surrender. Prophetically, I knew that all of my experiences: past, present, and future, were divinely assigned and positioned solely for my enlightenment. I can venture as deep and wide and ascend as far and high as I choose to, so long as I am willing to accept and surrender to whatever I am met.

Through what felt like death, I re-birthed myself—allowing Self to become a pure vessel and portal between the spiritual and physical realms. I did not realize I was doing birth work long before becoming a doula, but this was spiritual midwifery. I did all I felt led to do—I enrolled in self-development programs, journaled profusely as a form of healing, developed a yoga practice, started therapy, ran two half-marathons, and studied many religions in search of Self. I lived with and ultimately transcended Lyme Disease. I experienced and lost myself in many attachments—to situations, to people, to fantasies, and inevitably to disillusionment.

Deep in the trenches of my soul, I inquired into the

purpose of this life. My instructions came through exactly "type up your notes from various journals, and use those notes to form a book. These lessons are not yours alone. They must be shared." Bewildered by the request initially, I knew this assignment would eventually become my offering. Over time, I reviewed my notes, letters, and pleas that all took the form of time-stamped journal entries. I had written in six different journals—the pages and lessons spanning many cities and locations. I wrote under the trees in Atlanta, Georgia, and on top of mountains in Cape Town, South Africa; across bridges from Brooklyn to New Jersey; in the clouds while traveling cross-country, at the foot of the ocean in Malibu, on the floor of the temple in Lagos. In between sips of tea in London. Under the rising sun and the sounds of chanting prayers in Istanbul. In a treehouse in Mexico and on the grass in Washington, D.C.

As I reviewed the words and lessons communicated to me from *Source*, I admittedly still found some strands of self-doubt. I even found myself wondering if I were the one to share this information. If now was the right time. The feeling of wanting or fictitiously needing to accomplish more and establish credibility in hopes that I would find a sign or confirmation to give credence to what *Spir-*

it had communicated to me. It is human nature to be in a constant search for validation. Peace is getting to a place where I can quiet the noise and allow *Spirit* to be my validation. The Lineage of Love is an ode to the ancestors and a reflection on the evolution of my spiritual journey. I had been in a vicious fight for my life. Love has proven to be the great elixir, the remedy, the balm, and the root of many traditions and practices where I found solace.

"Where do I begin my spiritual journey?" A common inquiry to which I do not have an unequivocal answer. My hope is for this book to assist you through the spaces of your awakening. I speak about many modalities and metaphysical practices. May you find at least one to be a springboard for you, a catalyst for your healing. I know for me, the journey began with a resounding yes. When you commit to your yes, you begin to choose truth over illusion. You begin to ask and desire more from your experience in this earthly realm. With this sincere desire, you have given your higher self-permission to guide your path.

The ways we function and evolve inside this universal reality is a choice we must make with intention, firm commitment, and unyielding discipline. Be mindful of relinquishing power outside of yourself. Be vigilant of the myr-

Ẹ KÁÀBỌ WELCOME

iad of people showing up as healers, mediums, or guides offering you healing. Allow the transfiguration to happen within you. No one can heal you. Rest assured the individuals placed on your journey to provide guidance will be revealed to you. You will know when you encounter them as they are conduits on your path and to your healing.

As you grow through your journey, you will need to silence the noise and recognize your intuition. You will want to spend time in meditation to understand what *Spirit* feels like when communicating. You will need to discern the contraction and expansion of your energetic vibration. You will want to spend time grounded on earth with the trees, feet on the grass or the shore, at the foot of the ocean. You will need the fruits of the *Spirit*— love, joy, peace, patience, gentleness, goodness, faithfulness, and self-control. You will also need a carefully curated community and friendships to hold space for you. These consist of loved ones who will not always make you comfortable and yet remind you of your commitment. On your journey, do not be attached to who shows up or not. You cannot control how people contribute, but you must always remain in alignment with the law of reciprocity.

While your path is unique, there will always be a quintessential moment, time frame, or crisis that activates something in you. I liken it to a birthing person who reaches active labor. Your breathing becomes shallow, and pain can seem intolerable just before you transition and ascend to a higher version of Self. What feels communal is reconnecting to our ancestors' ways, for we are met with what they have faced, likely with more resources and more comforts than they were afforded. Inside each of us lies innate ancestral wisdom that can guide us, our families, and communities through this shift. It will be appropriate for you to bow, to touch your head to the floor for those who have come before you.

As our world shifts consciousness collectively, and as we metamorphose individually, many will transition from this life. For those who remain, we owe it to ourselves and those who have left to walk unapologetically in the truth of who we are. Less we forgo the evolution, only to repeat the same lessons over time.

There is no theory to be proven here. There are no debates to be had, and no one size fits all guide that will claim to get you through any particular juncture of life. Instead,

Ẹ KÁÀBỌ̀ WELCOME

I invite you into a collection of *Spirit* downloads, poems, journal entries, and musings influenced by deliberate walks and conversations with our Creator. You will also find references inspired by other books, authors, and experts that I have indulged along the way.

I am holding space for whatever it takes for you to get back to love. It may take loving yourself, indeed. It is altering your narrative and outdated conversations, healing trauma, honoring your ancestral lineage, forgiving yourself and reconnecting with your soul. For some, it will only require you to gather new tools and information to support you on this path to self-discovery. For others, a complete uproot will be necessary. Whatever it is, may you find a peace that leaves you feeling understood and seen in a massive world that can incidentally leave us feeling isolated.

I know that for many of us, our life has never felt like our own. I know that we only exist as and because of love. I know that only love is real. I know that love heals all things and transcends all things. I know that it is humbling and exuberant to be a messenger, allowing *Spirit* to move through me to write these words. We are on a lifelong journey that neither starts nor ends here because what I have learned to be true is that the beginning and the end are the same. There is no mountaintop! While I am not authorized to tell you where to begin, the *Spirit* vested in me requests I share the alchemy of our ancestors.

There is something new emerging. The revolution will not be televised because the revolution is within you. I trust that this text will find you, wherever you are on your journey, and wrap you tightly in the love that will grow you. Your strand can never be broken or lost. Your entire lineage is rooting for you.

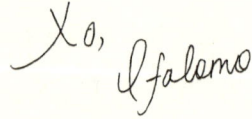

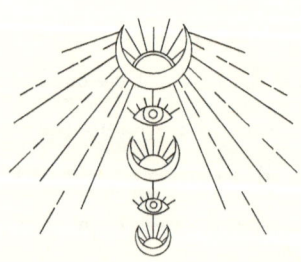

PART I

In the middle of an eclipse and retrograde season.
I do not know if I'm coming or going some days.
Things are moving slow, but things are certainly moving.
Traumas are being revealed. Ancestral traumas are being healed.
I am at most in the driver's seat of my healing and my creations.
And at the very least, I am getting 6-8 hours of sleep a night.
I'm introspective, and even my introspections are of retrospect.
I feel the love, even in my solitude.
I'm challenging the illusions I've made a reality.
I am loving on the voids I've historically tried to get others to fill.
I have so many creative ideas swirling.
I'm writing a lot.
I celebrated a solar return. I bought a house.
And I'm training for another half-marathon.
Still, somehow I feel like I'm just getting started.
I guess that's because there is no mountaintop.

[JOURNAL ENTRY 001:
THERE IS NO MOUNTAINTOP]

CHAPTER 1

THE WAY

> "YOU MUST FIND YOUR OWN WAY TO YOUR OWN TRUTH. FOR BEFORE EACH AND EVERY ONE OF YOU LIES YOUR PATHWAY, A DOORWAY, AN EYE OF THE NEEDLE, THROUGH WHICH ONLY YOU CAN FIT."
>
> THE WAY OF MASTERY, LESSON 4

THE LINEAGE OF LOVE

I have always considered myself an avid reader. Since my youth, I would get lost in books. There is still something fascinating to me about words and how they weave together to tell a story, create an image, and take you someplace. Trips to the library are a favorite pastime of mine. I had a Language Arts teacher in middle school who deepened my appreciation for and love of words, books, and stories. Typically, my read of choice is non-fiction, spiritual in nature, or perhaps an autobiography.

One evening, I was at a friend's house. She invited me to take a book home from her collection. I was immediately drawn to a blue book with gold writing titled *The Way of Mastery*, by the Shanti Christo Foundation. I am not exactly sure what drew me to the book; it felt like something I needed to read. As I reached for the book, I noticed my friend hesitate. She requested that I take any other book outside of that one. She shared how much of an impact it had on her life and could not fathom parting ways with it. She suggested I get a copy for myself, "You would not have been drawn to this book if you were not ready for it," she wisely shared. She was right; I picked an alternate book, and as soon as I got home, I went online and ordered my copy of *The Way of Mastery*. I thought it would be a relatively easy read. Instead, it had become a two-year journey into my beliefs, judgments, capacity to forgive, to create, and to love.

The Way of Mastery became one of the most profound books I ever read. Mostly because it was not just a book; it became a quest—a safe space for me to become the querent. As you continue to read the next few pages, you will find I share tons of notes from this authoritative text. *The Way of Mastery* consists of three sections: The Way of the Heart, The Way of Transformation, and the Way of Knowing. As I was completing the last section—The Way of Knowing, *Spirit* communicated with me to write this book to share my notes and insights in a way that could be grasped and understood by others. It was during the Way of Transformation that the healing powers we became heirs of when the Creator made us in her image became apparent. And, it was during The Way of the Heart that my ancestors began to speak so clearly, and direct my steps so evidently.

Brevity is essential to me, so I aim not to inundate you with information. If something resonates and piques an interest within you, I invite you to dig deeper. If a reference speaks to you, I implore you to read more on that

THE LINEAGE OF LOVE

topic. I included recommendations in the back of the book to support your deeper dive. I want to remind you that healing is not linear. You and I nor this book are linear. While I know that there are tons of ways to read a book, and how you indulge is your choice. I do want to suggest that you read from a very personal space of truth. While I share my own stories, I urge you to observe where you may be dealing with something similar. This reading experience is less about my story and more about finding your way home through my sharing.

Find yourself in these words. Allow yourself to become the querent. Pay attention to the feelings you get, the synchronicity that may be occurring in your life. Your

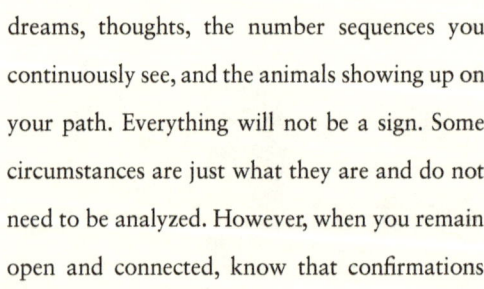

dreams, thoughts, the number sequences you continuously see, and the animals showing up on your path. Everything will not be a sign. Some circumstances are just what they are and do not need to be analyzed. However, when you remain open and connected, know that confirmations and signs will be abundant. You will learn to decipher these messages. Your guides are always speaking in their own unique way. As you pay close attention, you will understand the communication—my grandmother visits in the form of red cardinals.

As I was writing this book, I considered sharing writing prompts and steps to ignite your journey, ultimately I decided against it. We are living in such times where we have become dependent upon step-by-step guidelines from someone else's perspective and quick fixes to heal or to conjure up what we think will fulfill us— take this pill and voila. Turn to this page to guide you through this particular circumstance. The psychology of instant gratification is a powerful force. It's human nature to want things now, the cliff notes, the carefully curated images of the crystals and the sage without the internal work. My step two may be your step six, and your step four may not even be something your best friend is going to cover in this lifetime.

Allow your internal compass to lead. It will take time, and it may feel often like a scenic route. This feeling is most palpable when comparing your journey to that of others. There is reprieve in understanding that your internal compass will always guide you toward your unique destiny. To begin or deepen your practices, you must call on *Spirit*: *"Spirit, please help bring*

> "SPIRIT, PLEASE HELP BRING ME FORTH."

me forth." Be open to putting action and energy into what comes up. *Spirit* will always deliver. Life follows the energy of our focus and faith, which is essentially the energy of our desires and intention.

CONSIDER THE FOLLOWING QUESTIONS AS YOU JOURNEY:

— Who am I?
— How do I define love?
— How do I define source? What is Spirit?
— What is the foundation of my spiritual beliefs?
— Do they resonate completely with who I know myself to be?
— Who am I concerning my family?
— Who am I in relation to my soul?
— What do I truly desire?
— Are there any generational habits or patterns that I see myself taking on?
— Where is there dis-ease in my life?
— Where is there dis-ease in my body?
— Am I ready to let go of what "runs in my family?"

- Am I willing to continue the legacy of my lineage?
- Do I wish to continue in the current energy I find myself or should I chose something else?
- Am I willing to try things I have never tried to receive what I want?

Giving thought to these questions and practicing radical self-honesty is an excellent practice in accepting things as they are and as they come as opposed to how we imagine them. This practice defies the perception on how societal structures make us believe things should be. So breathe deeply. Straighten your spine. Give yourself a lot of space. Make some tea. Get your journal. Set your intention. And stay postured for a miracle.

spoiler alert

YOU ARE THE MIRACLE.

CHAPTER 2

COMING INTO BEING

"YOU THINK YOU ARE YOURSELF, BUT YOU REALLY ARE A BUNDLE OF REACTIVITY SEEKING TO FIND APPROVAL, SEEKING TO FIND SAFETY, SURVIVAL, FRIENDSHIP—IN THE WORLD. THAT IS, YOU ARE ALREADY CAUGHT UP IN THE PERCEPTION THAT WHAT YOU EXPERIENCE IS COMING TO YOU FROM THE OUTSIDE, AND THAT YOU MUST, THEREFORE, SEEK TO ADAPT YOURSELF TO IT. YOU ARE NOT YET ALIVE."

THE WAY OF MASTERY, LESSON 17

COMING INTO BEING

You are a field of energy, existing within a web of relationships. The first universe you experience within the physical dimension is the womb. In the womb, you were in constant communication with what was passing through your mother's energy field. As stated in *The Way of Mastery*, you experienced more than just the potpie she had for dinner or the coffee she drank that made your heart race. You also experience the air quality she breathes and all of the emotional energy she was experiencing in her universe—inclusive of her relationships, fears, trauma, joy, excitement, and her experience and perception of the world.

Before you are born, while in the womb, you are feeling, sensing, remembering, and being in your mother's energy field. You are also aware of the energy field of your father and any other immediate family members. The birth experience, therefore, significantly impacts who you will become. In *The Secret Life of the Unborn Child*, Dr. Thomas Verny details intriguing evidence on the impact of the parents' attitude in general toward the child and the pregnancy on the psychological development of the child. Not just mere fleeting thoughts that arise, but rather the deep, persistent patterns of feelings are the ones that are imprinted on your emotional development. Knowing this does not forego responsibility or allow blame to be placed on parents. It only highlights the reality that inside of each of us exists thoughts, feelings, and reality, not necessarily our own.

Habitual, emotional, mental, and mood patterns can run for hundreds of years down the genealogical trees of families from one generation to the next through epigenetics. These positions modify the DNA, becoming the default setting in the emotional center whenever there is a threat—whether real or imagined—in your environment. This becomes the lens through which you view the world. These memories and perceptions were sealed as you took your first breath. This view may be what is obstructing your journey toward self-actualization. It will be beneficial to become curious, perhaps even asking your parents what experiences shaped their reality. If you are not able to have the discussion with your parents, you can still become curiously engaged in your default habits, views, and thought processes. You will find them to be very revealing.

My work and training as a doula has gifted me with fleeting experiences and insight into my birth. Remembering your passage here is possible, and the ways to access these memories are abundant. Your cells hold conceivably vague memories of the past, present, and future. These memories allow you to age into adult form while still playing out the childhood fears, undissolved insecurities, attachment issues, and separation anxiety. Most of the problems you find yourself working through in this life is merely an extension of unhealed parental matters. Once you accept that your parents are also working through unresolved inner child issues—while doing the very best they can with the tools and knowledge they have available to them—then you will have the space to forgive and heal. You enabling Self to heal will do work to free up seven generations to come, as well as seven generations that precedes you. This is the power you have access to when you relinquish blame.

Everyone holds scars from their childhood— rich or poor, black or white, religious or atheist, active and pres-

---

YOU ENABLING SELF TO HEAL WILL DO WORK TO FREE UP SEVEN GENERATIONS TO COME, AS WELL AS SEVEN GENERATIONS THAT PRECEDES YOU.

---

ent parents, seemingly perfect or absent alike, and everything in between. These scars are more immeasurable than the knee scrape from when you fell off your bike or the mark under your eye you still have from rough playing. The wounds that penetrate deeply are often not shown physically; instead, they are the subtle beliefs that you are not enough, the often debilitating fear of abandonment, or the way you masterfully self-sabotage. Your parents did the work to bring you here. Ideally, they provided for you when you were unable to provide for yourself. The parent-child relationship is one where the role of teacher and student is infallibly blurred.

Wherever you find yourself inside of your relationship with your parents, know that no other two humans could have come together to form you precisely as you are. Who you are is perfect and, without error, an invaluable contribution to our planet. The work you do in this lifetime to heal is not meant to change who you are. It is intended for you to accept who you are. There will be potent

> **WHO YOU ARE IS PERFECT AND, WITHOUT ERROR, AN INVALUABLE CONTRIBUTION TO OUR PLANET.**

opportunities to grow. Once here on Earth, you are gifted an opportunity to labor and birth yourself at varying junctures of life.

As you birth yourself, understand that in her most natural form, the Self is a bundle of reactivity seeking to find comfort, safety, survival, and companionship in the physical world. Your earliest experiences with comfort came from outside of Self—food, safety, entertainment. Naturally, as you grow, you still seek to find something outside of yourself for fulfillment before working to retrieve it on the inside. Searching for happiness out there is a foregone conclusion until you reach a point where you turn inward and listen to the calling of your soul. Only then do you begin to activate the keys to the kingdom.

In the Yoruba spiritual system, Ifa, it is explained that we have chosen our heads while in heaven. The phrase "you have a good head on your shoulders" is the literal truth. Baba Adegun Iwindara Reece's book *ObaKaye Temple Field Manual* speaks of our head as our higher Self. This is called one's Ori. Your Ori holds the memories of your destiny; it is your personal God. You have an inner head accessed through the umbilicus/ navel concerned with desires. Aligning your destiny and desires while walking through the veil toward your truth is the divine rebirth.

Life shifts dramatically when you realize you do not exist by chance or outside of your deliberate choice to live in this body on this Earth. You were fashioned with intent, in the image of your Creator; therefore, there is nothing that has been established that you do not have access to.

Creating as God creates is, in fact, your birthright. Necessarily, if God is the sun, you are the sunbeams of the sun. If you equate God to the ocean, know that you are created from this water. Remembering on a cellular level who you are is what it means to settle into your truth.

This experience on Earth may not be your first one. Some advanced souls traveled here many times before. These souls have a sure discernment and wisdom about life that you only get with experience. In contrast, other souls are young and experiencing this realm for the first time. In heaven, you (the you that is your soul) chose to incarnate for precise reasons—to heal, elevate, contribute—to the lineage, to Earth, and to a specific community of people. Based on that promise, you chose to incarnate in the form you did. A woman or a man—depending on what there is to accomplish. You may choose to be a Black woman or a

Black man, an Asian woman, or an Indian man. You may even have chosen to be very rich or very poor.

You choose these identities because they are in direct alignment with the work you have come to complete. You also choose who you will incarnate through, so yes, you choose your parents from your lineage to fulfill your destiny. The promise could have been you go first, then I will incarnate through you. So, you have this nagging feeling of being the parent when you appear to be the child. It could have been to finish the work in the community that Rev. Dr. Martin Luther King, Jr. began. It could be to heal the trauma in your family that your grandmother could not complete before she transitioned. Or to bring forth the vision that your great-grandfather did not have the freedom to do or create. He may have been enslaved in his body, but now that reality has begun shifting, you arrived to share the dream, cultivate the land, or grow the family business. Coming into being is bringing your true Self to life. It becomes the gift of incessant rebirth.

Your destiny may be challenging to recall. The journey from the spiritual to the physical realm is likened to touching the tree of forgetfulness for most. Once you forget it then becomes easy to be molded into a social construct instead of receiving divination at birth to give insight into why this soul chose to incarnate. You were given a sort of checklist that includes all of the things you should accomplish to become externally successful. With this checklist in mind and the arbitrary questioning of adults, "What do you want to be when you grow up?" You create a path toward a career likely chosen based on what you've been exposed to or earning potential. When in actuality it is only through your connection to *Source* that you begin to fulfill on your purpose.

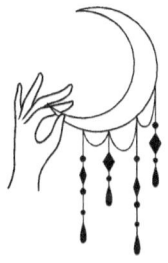

The moon was full that night, and we were preparing moon water.

As I gazed upward toward the moon, thinking of everything and nothing I could feel the high kicking in.

I looked over at her; she was high too.

I felt her words forming before she spoke, "you need to let yourself breathe!" I questioned, "you think I'm not breathing?"

She said, "no. you are not"

So how am I alive? I thought, the words slowly came out.

"So... how... am... I... alive?"

She said, "You aren't alive. You are just existing because your brain won't let you kill yourself."

HOW...AM...
I...ALIVE?

[JOURNAL ENTRY 002:
HOW AM I ALIVE?]

CHAPTER 3

POWER SOURCE

> "YOU WERE BIRTHED TO BE GRAND.
> YOU WERE BIRTHED FOR GREATNESS.
> YOU WERE BIRTHED TO SHINE FORTH
> SUCH LIGHT INTO THIS WORLD THAT
> THE WORLD REMEMBERS THAT LIGHT
> IS TRUE, AND DARKNESS IS ILLUSION.
> BE YOU, THEREFORE, THAT WHICH
> YOU ARE—YOU ARE THE LIGHT OF THE
> WORLD."
>
> THE WAY OF MASTERY, LESSON 4

ource is a generative force that supplies information. To access power in an electronic device, we have to plug a cord into the outlet, or the power source. The same goes for all spiritual beings having a human experience. You maximize the full potential of your experience by plugging into the power source.

Many refer to *Source* as a name that resonates with their beliefs, culture, language, or geographical region—God, Olodumare, Allah, Ra, Yahweh, the Universe—we are all speaking to and of the same Supreme Creator. The Almighty. The Most High. The immeasurable, undefined, omnipotent, ever-present force responsible for all of creation.

You either spend your life consciously connected to *Source*, or subconsciously searching for a connection to *Source*. Because you are an extension of *Source*, you can rest assured that there is nothing you need to do to get to *Source*. However, there may be much to undo for *Source* to get to you.

In this text, I use *Source* and *Spirit* interchangeably. To clarify, granted that we exist in human form in the physical, we are ultimately spirits. There is a nonphysical part of each of us that is the seat of emotion and character; the soul. The nonphysical part of a person comes from and returns to *Source*—the ether, cosmos, heaven, the astral plane or realm, the vastness of the universe undefined by space or time.

There is an ancient motto I use often '*as above, so below*,' deriving from a passage in *The Emerald Tablet* "That which is Below is like that which is Above and that which is Above is like that which is Below, to accomplish the miracle of the One Thing." The phrase indicates that what happens on one level of reality is also happening on all other levels. What is being lived in the microcosm of earthly matters exists in the macrocosm of heavenly matters. Therefore, there is no separation between Self and Soul, the lower and the higher, the living and the dead. This truth is also rendered in the *Lord's Prayer* from *Matthew 6:10* "thy kingdom come, thy will be done. On earth as it is in heaven." Before we exist on earth we existed in heaven, and when we die we return to heaven, what is often left unmentioned is our existence simultaneously in both realms.

You were created in physical form to fulfill the destiny and mission of the soul. As you incarnate in human form, your soul is ever present in your body and tethered to the ether from which you originated. As you journey from esoteric to exoteric, you are assigned guides to aid in the fulfillment of your destiny.

Spirit guides are the plugs that connect you directly to the power source. They have transcended this realm, becoming elevated beings capable of guiding, protecting, and interceding on our behalf in the heavenly realms. Our *Spirit* guides are the Orisa, the enlightened masters like Jesus, Buddha, Krishna, Muhammad, our ancestors (egungun) and our heavenly mates (egbe). Any living being that has transitioned from Earth is considered an ancestor. Your ancestors are those from your direct lineage, and extends to those in your communities. Our remembrance and veneration of this collective force ensures them a place among the living.

> SPIRIT GUIDES ARE THE PLUGS THAT CONNECT YOU DIRECTLY TO THE POWER SOURCE.

When you allow yourself to experience the real power of *Source*, you will begin to understand there are many paths. You must find the path that allows you the strongest and most reliable connection based on your particular values and your unique destiny. You can liken yourself to a device. There is one universal power source, but not every plug will work for every device. If you have ever traveled outside of your country or region, perhaps to a European or African country, you would have quickly noticed your standard plug would not fit the outlet without a converter. In the absence of a knowledgeable understanding of your device and the specific outlet it needs to function, you never fully tap into your power, thus you are unable to reach your full potential.

All else flows from your connection to *Source*.

CHAPTER 4

SUBSTANCE OF THINGS
HOPED FOR

"WHEN YOUR ONLY DESIRE IS LOVE, YOU WILL BE WILLING TO SET ANYONE FREE, TO SUPPORT HIM OR HER ON THEIR OWN JOURNEY, NO MATTER WHAT IT IS OR WHAT IT TAKES. YET, YOU WILL NEVER FEEL YOUR LOVE WAVER."

THE WAY OF MASTERY, LESSON 6

THE LINEAGE OF LOVE

When my paternal Grandmother, Julia Catherine Dickerson passed away, the dreams I had of her *Spirit* transitioning were vivid. I was nineteen years old at the time. My family picked me up from Meridian Hill Hall, my dorm room at Howard University. We were headed south to North Carolina to bid farewell to one of my absolute favorite human beings. I was distraught. Two years before her transition during my senior year of high school, my Grandmother suffered a brain aneurysm and never quite recovered. I had numbed myself in the interim, but her death was still very jarring. I did not have the tools nor the language to process the grief.

The night of Grandma Julia's viewing, I was restless. Somewhere between tears, I finally drifted off to sleep. It was there that my Grandmother met me in a dream. In the dream, I was visited by what I interpreted to be God. It was not a person but a force, a bright light. Almost blinded by the intensity of the light, I could feel myself backing away as I heard a voice calling out to me, and I saw my Grandmother ascending into the light—with her signature red lipstick and lips pursed. My Grandmother reached her hand out toward me as the light began to swallow her in. I tried reaching back for her, but my body was heavy, I could not move. I felt the tears on my face and the subtle reassurance that she was to transition alone. I still had more to do. The voice called out, "your connection will never die. It only changes form." I woke up inconsolable and comforted at the same time—the *Spirit* of who I came to know as Grandma Julia returned to the Creator.

Having insight into my Grandmother's transition and the forewarning that our love never dies did not assuage the pain I felt, which later turned into anger and disillusionment. The morning after my mystic experience, the funeral and the burial took place. I sat in silence as the casket containing my Grandmother's physical body was lowered to the Earth. *"She is not here; She is risen"* a verse from Matthew 28, replayed in my head. I would hear this scripture of Jesus' resurrection often during the Lenten season. Here we are in early December, and I am experiencing a version of what I have read. I thought I would just stay there at the foot of her burial site forever. Everyone had begun to

> "SHE IS NOT HERE; SHE IS RISEN"

make their way back to their respective vehicles. My maternal Grandmother Arletha 'Grandma Lee' Wilkins came to be with me. She helped me up and walked me to the car in her arms. I could not understand how life was intended to go on. Grandma Lee promised me that it would, "it won't be the same, but you still have me." I sobbed in her arms.

The days and months that followed my Grandmother's transition were a blur. I do not recall returning to school or even what we did for the Christmas holiday that year. I was numb. All I knew to be true was that our physical experience on Earth is just a fraction of what we experience. I felt that I belonged to two worlds—a physical one and a spiritual one. The astuteness of the spiritual realm offered a transcendental journey to various mystical spaces. I spent my days in a daze, at a gateway between two worlds, rarely present and barely awake.

It is painful to lose the physical body of a loved one, but what was missing for me until this moment was the truth that memories are not all that we have left. As the container that holds the soul, the body at some point ceases to be beneficial, the soul transcends, and the relationship we had takes a new form. After my Grandmother passed, I tip-toed around her death. The gravity of her absence in the physical felt too heavy, so my coping mechanism became dissociation. I never revisited the site of her grave. I did not do anything to commemorate the date of her death nor her birth. Every year around the time of her passing, I would feel extreme sadness. One evening, almost ten years since she transitioned, I realized I could no longer hear her voice. How is it that I still remembered her old landline number, but I could not recall her voice? I cried myself to sleep. Grandma Julia visited me in a dream that night, I heard her voice clearly and felt the comfort of her presence. I knew then that my Grandmother had been there all along. She had never left me. The moment I called out to her with a request, she answered. Our angels have names and distinctive ways to communicate. We need them to navigate, and they need us as well.

I will, with the assistance of my guides become aware of my personal needs, wants, thoughts and feelings and I will honor that, forever. I will honor this out of respect and love of self, and I will honor it in reverence of those that surrendered.

I will honor it in reverence of those whose submission allowed for me have a say, a choice. I will radically honor those on the ancestral realm for their bravery, their foresight, their love, their strength.

I give thanks. Thank you!

Thank you, God. Thank you, Jesus. Thank you, Orisa. Obatala. Angels. Spirits. Fairies. Warriors. Healers. Deities.

Thank you, Rachel Manley and those that took on the role of a slave.

Thank you, Gracie, Jasper, Albert, Julia, Ernell, Edward Sr. Ella Lee.

Thank you, Maya, Martin, Malcolm, Paul, Langston, Gwendolyn, Zora, Fred, Harriet, Sojourner, Nat.

Thank you James Baldwin, Uncle Jimmy.

Thank you, Trayvon. Thank you, Amadou.

For those that I have omitted, I thank you.

For those whose name I do not know, I thank you, and I ask that you reveal yourself to me. With love, reverence, and gratitude.

I got you.

Ase'

[JOURNAL ENTRY 003 : AN ODE TO THE ANCESTORS]

CHAPTER 5

RELIGIOUS PURSUITS

"SELF-LOVE IS THE PERFECTION OF ALL SPIRITUAL PRACTICE. SELF-LOVE IS THE FINAL, SHINING RAY OF LIGHT THAT ILLUMINATES THE HEART OF THE INDIVIDUATED RAY OF LIGHT THAT YOU ARE. SELF-LOVE TRANSFIGURES THE MIND, THE EMOTIONAL BODY, AND EVEN THE PHYSICAL BODY TO THE DEGREE THAT IT STRONGLY SHINES INTO THE CELLS OF THE BODY."

THE WAY OF MASTERY, LESSON 34

THE LINEAGE OF LOVE

When I was ten years old, I insisted on going to the church in our Brooklyn neighborhood. I found out one of my classmates sang in the children's choir, and I wanted in. My mother consented, she and I began going to the church together. One Sunday morning, after the sermon, I felt a deep sensation to respond to the altar call. I honored my intuition, maneuvering through the pew, past some of my choir member friends, and up to the altar to accept Jesus Christ as my Lord and Savior. Deep down, I wanted to feel safe. I wanted my family and me to be protected. Over the next three years, my siblings and Dad began coming to church with my Mom and me. Eventually, we were all baptized together. My consolation was knowing that we would all meet again in the afterlife if any of us left earth prematurely. The church is the foundation from which I have grown and cultivated my spirituality.

As I grew of age, particularly when I took my first trip to the African continent, my views and ideologies began to shift. Questions about the root of Christianity emerged that I had not grappled with before. I traveled to Senegal, where I spent time in Dakar and in a small village named Djinack Barra, seven hours outside of Dakar near the Gambian border. We arrived in Djinack Barra by boat, the images of the bright colors that awaited us at the shore are forever etched in my memory. The children welcomed us with a dance and lively drumming while the elders prepared Thieboudienne, a traditional Senegalese dish made with fish, rice, and vegetables.

The people of Djinack Barra did not have very much materially, they had to travel to a well to fetch clean water, but they were rich in spirit, community, tradition, and love. They shared themselves with us so generously and so graciously. I fell in love with the souls of the people there. Even with the language barriers, the sincere gratitude and purity of heart were palpable.

My last morning in Djinack, I sat on the side of the road and enjoyed a game of mancala and a cup of tea with Insa Sonka, a son of the island, before heading back to Dakar. During the bus ride to Dakar, in all of my gratitude, I sat in reflection of such a fulfilling encounter. My thoughts were fleeting yet unyielding, mostly conflicted with the Christian notion that no one can get to the Father except through Christ. Djinack Barra was a Muslim village, most of the Senegalese that I have encountered submitted to the Islam faith. The concept of needing to make it into heaven had become a fixation for me, so much so that it was limiting my experience of the fullness of earth. I could not fathom these beautiful souls being excluded from heaven due to their culture and place on the planet.

Back in Dakar, our tour guide Sineta took us to visit the Door of No Return on Gorée Island. The door symbolizes the many enslaved Africans that passed through as they boarded ships during the Transatlantic Slave Trade. The mood at the Maison des Esclaves (house of slaves) was swampy and somber. The gentle sea breeze and the laughter of children playing in the ocean a few feet away could not veil the heaviness of the atmosphere. The catholic church that stood to the left of the slave house further conflicted me. My thoughts from the days prior deepened: What was the church's role during the transatlantic slave trade? I became suspicious of anything taught to enslaved beings by their oppressor, namely religion.

In the space that led to the Door of No Return, we stood in a damp room with low ceilings and a small slit for a window when a sudden weakness overtook my knees. The space around me was spinning, my head was light, and I felt an uneasiness in my throat. The tour guide who accompanied us explained that enslaved Africans who did not meet the weight requirement for the long trip ahead were force-fed in the room we stood. She recommended I step out for fresh air. Once outside, the sensations subsided, but not the melancholy. I had always had the gift of clairsentience, the uncanny ability to acquire knowledge by means of feeling. Senegal seemed to deepen my propensity to feel.

Since Senegal, I have studied many religions in search of Self. Islam was a short stint because it felt restrictive for me. The most beautiful and pure souls I have met on this earth are followers of Islam and many students of the Honorable Elijah Muhammad. With gratitude to Islam, I learned discipline, self-control, and the importance of community. Nevertheless, it was not the practice to root myself in. Contrastingly, Buddhism, particularly the Soka Gakkai community, was among the most peaceful, liberating, and mindful spiritual practices. I feel deep support all around me and peace throughout me as I chant Nam-myoho-renge-kyo—a pledge to oneself to never yield to difficulties and to win over one's suffering. It was at the Buddhist Center that the power of collective prayer resonated. Chanting helped me to the other side of suffering. It taught me loving detachment, non-violence, and acceptance of all circumstances. Having the privilege to experience different cultures and spiritual systems is a gift I hold in high regard. I find the common thread in these practices to be love.

Something that has always been missing for me along my spiritual journey was my ancestors' inclusion. I had a deep interest in my ancestors' precolonial spiritual practices. I wanted to explore African spirituality without needing to validate my belief in Christ or defend my choice. Western culture demonizes the idea of venerating ancestors in a ritualistic way. I do presume this is by design. I was walking Morehouse College campus with my mentor and pastor, Rev. Dr. Mark V.C. Taylor, on one of his visits to Atlanta. We were conversing deeply as we do, on an array of topics from life choices and friendship to the African Diaspora. I shared my growing interest in traditional African spiritual systems, particularly the Yoruba system, Ifa, to which he asked, "*What will you do with your Christianity?*" "Well, I plan to keep the parts that resonate and unlearn the parts that feel oppressive," I reassured. I knew my most challenging questions would come from this conversation. Instead of challenging me, he recommended some literature to indulge in and expressed interest in hearing more about my discoveries. I did not know what I would discover, but what I knew for sure was my personal freedom hinged upon me exploring the calling of my soul.

As it pertains to religion, I have a deep reverence for faith-based practice. The Church of the Open Door, my home church on the corner of Gold and Nassau Street was everything I needed the Black church to be—a safe space, an anchor in the middle of the housing projects, an advocate for the people, an activist for social justice, and a place for summer employment. Every mosque, temple, or spiritual center I set foot in was doing the community work they had been called to do. They each contributed to me standing on the truth of which I incarnated. This truth called on me to release myself from the belief that anything outside of Self could save me. My interpretation of the rules, the commandments, and the judgment day only contributed to my sense of lack, my dissonance on a cellular level, and ultimately to dis-ease in my body. Self-love then became the perfection and the maturation of all spiritual practices. Religion became expanding and undoing, becoming and unbecoming, and learning to love me without condition.

After all, how could a being, no matter how devout or

THE LINEAGE OF LOVE

faithful, ever come to love the Creator while rejecting her Creations. Any part of Self that is rejected is essentially a rejection of the Creator. Many can get to this place inside of the religion you have come to learn. My journey required an inevitable resurrection and awakening that took me beyond what felt safe. If I were speaking in Hov a/k/a Jay-Z, my journey took me fresh out of the frying pan into the fire.

> **ANY PART OF SELF THAT IS REJECTED IS ESSENTIALLY A REJECTION OF THE CREATOR.**

CHAPTER 6

EVIDENCE OF THINGS NOT SEEN

"THEREFORE, UNDERSTAND THAT YOU ARE AN EXTRAORDINARY BEING. YOU, RIGHT WHERE YOU ARE, ARE GIVEN OPPORTUNITIES MOMENT TO MOMENT TO BE THE TRUTH OF WHO YOU ARE, AND THEREFORE, BE THE LIGHT THAT LIGHTS THE WORLD. YOU ARE PART OF AN ANCIENT LINEAGE THAT STRETCHES BACK TO BEFORE CREATION BEGAN. THAT STRAND OF LIGHT HAS NEVER BEEN BROKEN OR LOST."

THE WAY OF MASTERY, LESSON 34

"Do you know about numerology?" my Uber driver asked as I was getting into the car. He had not even made eye contact with me yet. I thought what an interesting way to begin the conversation. "I do have an interest in numbers. I know the basics of numerology. What makes you ask?" I inquired. "As you were walking out of the building, there was a white light that resembled a halo over you. I turned to my phone, the time was 4:44 pm. Did you notice the address of the building you were coming out of?" he asked. Perhaps he noticed me lost in contemplation before I got the chance to respond, he interjected, "the building number was 444."

He went on to tell me that I had a hedge of protection around my family and me. He talked more about the significance of angel numbers before recommending that I read Psalm 91 twice a day for seven days. He said that I had angels fighting to protect me, and as long as I uphold a spirit of honor, nothing will harm me. The conversation then veered to his personal life and a custody battle he was in the midst of. Before he finished sharing, we had already reached my destination. I thanked him before rushing into the airport.

As soon as I got settled on the airplane, I read Psalm 91. I sent it to my family to read as well. The Psalms are incantations I recited it daily because the message was clear and the words comforting. In all things, I am protected. Our angels will speak to us in dreams, in symbols, and through divine messengers. My Uber driver, that afternoon in Richmond, Virginia, was a divine messenger. Through our brief interaction, I desired to know more intimately the angels fighting to protect me.

The veil between the *Spirit* realm and the living is thin. Once you begin calling your ancestors by name and creating a practice to honor and venerate them, you begin to remember who you are, and your life begins to unfold. You become privy to their wisdom and knowledge. They are your first line of defense and steadfast shoulders to plant yourself upon.

> **THE VEIL BETWEEN THE SPIRIT REALM AND THE LIVING IS THIN.**

Not long after the trip to Richmond, two friends invited me to attend a Soul Constellation session. I had never heard of it before the thrilling three-way call I received after their session. Something about the experience prompted them to reach out. They thought I would benefit from being a part of the conversation.

The Soul Constellation or Family Constellation is a practice from the South African Zulu Nation. It was introduced in America by a German psychotherapist named Bert Hellinger through his training with African Shaman Credo Mutwa. Soul Constellation recognizes that there are hidden dynamics at the root of any internal issue related to self, family, and community. Constellation refers to a group or cluster of related things. Unresolved issues and traumas can linger in families and communities for seven generations. The Soul Constellation intends to guide you through uncovering the root of a problem, ultimately releasing the stuck energies and patterns that may result in trauma, fear, or an inability to move forward in life. The work takes form using what scientists call the morphogenetic field, the dynamic, energetic field that connects all beings from the past, present, and future. It is the same field that allows you to think of someone and hear from them a few moments later. We charge it to coincidence; in reality, thoughts travel at light speed and are received instantaneously when you are open and present to this energetic field. You then understand that there is no such thing as coincidence.

Dr. Mark Armstrong facilitated my first Constellation at the Ahimki Center for Wholeness, a very gifted brother who has become a trusted friend and guide on my path. While the session is facilitated, the actual work plays out among the participants in the morphogenetic field. We poured libation and called out the names of ancestors—personal and community—the environment was peaceful. I did not envisage how the session would go in advance of my arrival. I was there wholly open to a new and life-changing experience. During the session, I uncovered a fit of deep-seated anger repressed within me since the transition of my Grandma Julia. I did not realize that I had been upset with my Grandmother for leaving us prematurely. Acknowledging the grief was heart-opening, I wrote a letter to her that night. The practice of communicating ignited a magnitude of peace and courage. I felt as if my ancestors were celebrating my acknowledgment of their role in my life.

I learned as many names from both my maternal and paternal lineage. I began to ask questions of the living elders on their interests and life stories. I would collect photos whenever I ventured to North Carolina for visits. My ancestors were guiding me, and it became quite an honor for me to learn about them and the parts of them that exist within me.

My paternal grandfather, Edward Dickerson, Jr., told me that I reminded him of his mother, Gracie (Wooten) Dickerson. He said whenever he saw me, he would think of his mother. I have met my great-grandmother, but I do not have a recollection. He told me that she was dedicated

to spirituality and read the Bible front to back. Grandma Gracie was a Bishop. She founded a church in Selma, North Carolina- Mt. Livingstone United Holy Church in the 1960s. I am confident that my faith and my pull toward

the Church had everything to do with Grandma Gracie. I explore and use my inner compass, my Ori, to guide me to what is ideal for my destiny. I know that my Ori will always veer me toward the ways of my lineage.

In my home, I set up an ancestral altar to honor those who have made it possible for my existence. I display photos of my ancestors along with a few items that had significance to them— a map of North Carolina and Brooklyn, a bible, and a bowl of water. I offer a portion of my meal, alcohol, flowers, or even coffee. I know that my home and the land on which it sits is a bestowal from my ancestors. I know because I can feel their presence, and because this particular home called to me, I did not seek it out. I surrendered to the pull that this was where I was supposed to be. I later learned the community I reside in was one the earliest communities inhabited by freed Africans. Everything they needed existed through indigenous resources. The land initially belonged to the Ingram family. Both my maternal and paternal Grandmothers are Ingrams'.

When I remark on lineage, I speak with profound honor and a deep reverence for those who have walked this Earth before me, including those who show themselves in my life daily. If you want to move your story forward, take the time to dissolve the curses that may have plagued your family for generations and welcome the gifts that are your birthright. I encourage you to start a loving relationship with those beings we call ancestors. You will repeat their lessons and fight the same fights if you do not consult them for strength, guidance, and truth.

Resurrection: The revitalization or revival of something.

Today I am particularly reflective on the journey of my honorable ancestors. I am grateful for the influence of both my maternal and paternal lineage.

The blood that flows through my veins is their blood—

Julia. Albert. Edward. Gracie. Walter. Lillie Mae. Ernell. Jasper. Ella. The Ingram's (twice over) The Dickersons. The Kings. The Wootens. The Ruffins. The Wilkins'. The Jones'. I am reflecting on those names and the names I do not know.

Easter or Resurrection Sunday is a holiday that I do not necessarily observe as I may have in the recent past. Instead, I honor it newly, I honor my ancestors, whose faith was rooted in Christianity.

I am a traditionalist, an Ifa devotee by choice. It is my path, and it was the path of my Yoruba foremothers and my forefathers. But not the ones that I can name. The ancestors whom names I call, offer libation and make offering to were devout followers of Jesus. Grandma Gracie had her church in Selma, North Carolina. Grandpa Albert always had his bible on hand. I will always honor, respect, and protect the traditions of my grandparents; this is my spiritual foundation, my help, and my comfort.

Today I asked my ancestors for their support as I navigate my internal compass and fulfill my destiny.

In their honor, I kneeled before my ancestral altar. I prayed. I read aloud from the book of Ecclesiastes. I lit a candle, and I prepared a meal— black-eyed peas. Mac n cheese. Cabbage. And hot water cornbread. I made an offering to them. My folk comes from North Carolina, so I chose a meal to appease them. My meal was the vegan version, it was yummy, and it didn't compromise the way I have come to prefer my food to be prepared.

I feel honored and empowered to find myself inside my tradition, my known and experienced southern traditions, and my intuitive and spiritual rituals. I am immensely connected to the responsibility and the gift it is to hold sacred seven generations from the past while preparing and holding space for seven generations to come.

The prayers of my ancestors are the wings that carry me.

On this particular Resurrection Sunday, I stand in awe of the revitalization and revival of traditionalism with profound and unyielding gratitude for the teachings of Jesus Christ. I have never felt more rooted in my truth or more connected to my lineage. Asè.

[JOURNAL ENTRY 004: RESURRECTION]

PART II

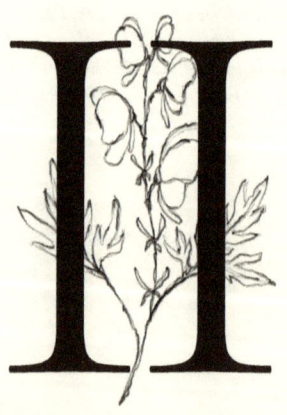

CHAPTER 7

KEYS TO THE KINGDOM

"YOU SEEK INNOCENCE AND PEACE. YOU SEEK ABUNDANCE, PROSPERITY, AND JOY. BUT OFTEN, WHEN YOU TOUCH THESE THINGS, IT FRIGHTENS YOU. WHY? BECAUSE THE TRUTH OF THE KINGDOM REQUIRES OPENNESS, TRUST, EXPANSIVENESS, AND SPACIOUSNESS. IT INVOLVES ALLOWING, TRUSTING, WITNESSING, AND LETTING THINGS COME AND GO. IT INVOLVES LEARNING TO CULTIVATE A DEEP ENJOYMENT OF WHATEVER ARISES, SEEING THAT ALL THINGS ARE JUST MODIFICATIONS OF CONSCIOUSNESS ITSELF, AND THEN LETTING THEM GO WHEN IT IS TIME TO DO SO."

THE WAY OF MASTERY, LESSON 2

THE LINEAGE OF LOVE

The Way of Mastery recommends a practice I found purposeful. Upon waking before doing anything else, ask yourself this simple question, "What do I truly desire?" This exercise does not require you to think or to try to answer the question. You simply ask and allow any spontaneous thought, feeling, or vision to come to you. You may desire to have a productive day, or an old friend comes to mind with whom you wish to reconnect. Maybe you want to stay in bed or simply brush your teeth. The desires are endless and limitless. There is nothing we do in life that does not begin with a desire.

Your mind may have traveled to the parts of your life you do not find enjoyable. When you trace the seemingly unenjoyable, you will still find the desire. Your job may not be considered satisfying, but the desire to make money resolves to this place of employment as a means to an end. Furthermore, you may desire to be comfortable and safe, avoiding risk, so you become frightened by a career or lifestyle that interferes with your comfort.

Knowledge is an integral part of defining and accessing the keys to the kingdom. Knowing our deepest desires as they arise and understanding the manifestation of hidden desires is the beginning of understanding God's will.

It is the desire that links us to the will of God. You are unable to desire anything that you have not been created to experience.

One of the first scriptures I learned was Hebrews 11:1 *"faith is the substance of things hoped for, the evidence of things not seen."* When I first examined faith, I had this misconception that it could only exist in the absence of fear. I thought enduring faith was something that I should innately have if I were a believer. Faith exists in the face of fear and uncertainty in actuality, and it continuously grows and strengthens with exercise.

Life enables us to gain endurance in faith by pressing upon the seat of our soul many lofty desires without a clue how they will come to fruition or what sort of personal transformation would be required to become the person who ushers it into fruition. You get the call from *Spirit* at seemingly the most inopportune times— do that, move to this city, go to that school, have the baby, visit this country by yourself, change your career, start that business, write this book. These moments offer you a grand opportunity to shrink or to expand in accordance with your faith. The faith exercise is trusting and allowing your ultimate desire to inch ahead of the fear. Understanding that without interference, fear becomes crippling, eradicating the realization of the desire with an influx of gut-wrenching yet nonsensical what-ifs.

The maturation of desire is intention. When you set an intention, everything involved in your being is integrated, working together, and focused on this grand desire. Because we are complicated humans with vast thoughts, resources, and needs, it is quite possible and common to lose sight of what we intended. Therefore our subconscious mind is creating intentions in opposition to what we want in reality.

You desire to express your creativity, so you begin drawing, writing, or creating music. At some point, you become discouraged because you cannot foresee making any money. Making money is now in direct opposition to you expressing your creativity. You have subconsciously collapsed these two desires in the stage of intention by creating a distraction.

Intention is applied by using your time and words constructively. Your actions will follow suit. Again, if you desire to hone your creative gifts, it is best cultivated through your intention to create. Distractions are inevitable. You can train yourself to become vigilant as distractions arise.

When you have committed yourself to complete an artistic piece by the end of the day, you get an invitation to go to the beach. You love the beach, so it feels comfortable, almost natural to veer from your intention and, ultimately, your desire. You may even tell yourself that a beach day will inspire your creativity. Whatever makes you feel better about the temporary distraction from your ultimate desire.

Dis-ease is created in the body and the reality of our daily lives when intentions are not clear. It is essential to often spend time in solitude to be clear on your desires, needs, and commitments. I have learned that isolation could hold different meanings for different people. I indulge in solitude through social media breaks, being in nature, allowing my feet to connect directly with the earth, or adopting a breathing practice that grounds me like meditation, qigong, or yoga. Detoxing my body, resting, or being single and doing the internal work when losing myself in a relationship or cause feels more comfortable. Whatever your choice may be, allow yourself to disconnect from the many information streams and connect deeply with Self. When deeply connected to Self, you can quiet the distractions and create what is in alignment with your unique desires and destiny.

Desire and intention together make way for allowance. Allowance is giving up control and attachment to your desire and intentions. We are wired to be doers, looking for ways to manipulate and control our environments to fulfill our desires. The keys to the kingdom are not inclusive of our egoic desires. Our egoic desires are rooted in looking good—achieving something of status that we believe will add prestige, happiness, or security to our lives. Allowance does not mean to strive or force. It is the cultivation of looking at your life events as stepping stones and not as obstacles to receiving what you want. In the stage of allowance, we begin to cultivate an acceptance of all things in our experience.

Allowance is accepting that because you already made the commitment, had the desire, and set the intention, you have a host of help conspiring to give you what you need. It is the understanding that individuals and events will show up to assist you with achieving your desires. These messengers also provide you with what you need to learn and become more aware of as your desires are made manifest.

The messenger can be a lover who entered your life and reached a place in your heart not formerly reached.

You feel so inspired by the love that you begin to tap into creativity and artistic abilities that were not available to you before this experience. Or you feel so broken by the void of the unmet expectations in the relationship that you finally turn inward, learning to nurture yourself.

The Way of the Heart describes allowance as the recognition that you must finally submit to something beyond the intellect and control of the egoic part of the mind. This is because you, the I, the maker and doer who has been trying to do it all is finally recognized as being inadequate. This realization leads to surrender, the final key.

Surrender is a lot like Luke 22:42. "Father, if you are willing, please take this cup of suffering away from me. Yet I want your will to be done, not mine." It is the willingness and the humility to recognize that while you are the leader of your life, your very existence is micro. You see only what is before you, but your Ori, the *Spirit* of the Living God, is what allows you to see further, have a knowing, and access the vastness of the totality of the life that you prayed for. Even the master visualizers, channelers, and astral travelers are required to rely on *Spirit* and be in constant surrender to the uninterrupted connection to the power of the all-knowing *Source*.

The keys to the kingdom are desire, intention, allowance, and surrender. The knowledge and awareness of desire set forth creation. Intention puts our desires into motion. Allowance is the willingness to be the recipient of what is needed to bring our creation to life, and surrender is a stage of perfect peace. Surrender is enjoying the journey and experiencing the fullness of your desires while knowing you may never receive an Oscar for your acting. Your best pieces may never be displayed at the Museum of Modern Art, yet you create anyway.

> **THE KEYS TO THE KINGDOM ARE DESIRE, INTENTION, ALLOWANCE, AND SURRENDER.**

Your journey, your pathway, and your way to mastery will be solely yours. It will look different than mine. It will look different from those closest to you. It may even look different from what you envisioned. Surrender is being contented in the moment and understanding you are the altar that you must kneel before. The keys to the kingdom gives you access to your power. Your power lies in accepting yourself fully while willingly sacrificing the parts of you that must die.

CHAPTER 8

LIBERATING DESIRE

"THE BODY ITSELF IS NO LONGER SEEN OR PERCEIVED AS SOMETHING THAT CAN BRING LOVE TO IT, OR CAN REACH OUT AND ATTRACT OR DRAW TO ITSELF WHAT HAS BEEN PERCEIVED AS VALUABLE IN THE WORLD. RATHER, THE BODY BECOMES ONE THING: A TEMPORARY OPPORTUNITY TO EXTEND THE GOOD, THE HOLY, AND THE BEAUTIFUL. IN OTHER WORDS, EVEN THE BODY ITSELF CAN HAVE NO PURPOSE, SAVE THAT WHICH THE COMFORTER, THE HOLY SPIRIT, THE RIGHT-MINDEDNESS WITHIN YOU, WOULD GIVE IT."

THE WAY OF MASTERY, LESSON 19

THE LINEAGE OF LOVE

Your experience of life is a direct reflection of your innermost feelings and thoughts. True peace, love, joy, abundance, security, evolution, and happiness is your birthright. When you find these eternal gifts are escaping you, it is a sure disconnection from *Source*. No accomplishment will guarantee you these foundations because none of the things you do or accomplish materially matter if they are not aligned with the mission of your soul.

Qualifying material accomplishments as a badge of honor or measure of success are norms of a capitalist society. It is often late in life or at the brink of death or tragedy that you realize none of your material gains is an accurate valuation of success or evidence of life well-lived. There is no marker that you must achieve to attain what already exists internally and eternally.

If you are unwilling to do the soul work, all of these possessions put you in a perpetual cycle of nothingness. Eventually, people get tired of living in that cycle. People start to tap out, step out and depend on things—a new title, a new mate, a lover, an addiction to escaping through food, sex, travel, drugs, or substances to get them through. Unfortunately, other people tap out entirely and take their own lives after acquiring the things they thought would fulfill them, only to find emptiness there too.

In this state of illusion, depression runs rampant, and discontentment is inevitable. Happiness becomes an objective that will surely be ours once we hit the next benchmark. These benchmarks, however, are illusions. They are inaccurate measurements. Contrary to societal norms and popular beliefs, happiness is not a plausible constant, nor is it a destination. It is a choice to be made on a moment to moment basis. The longing for anything outside of Self is a longing for *Source*.

Desiring things and acquiring things is not an issue. We were reminded in the Keys to the Kingdom that desire links us to the will of God. However, when your desire is single-minded and obsessive in nature, there is rarely space for *Spirit* to reveal or affirm your destiny. If you want to remember your birthright, it would greatly benefit you to question the significance of your material and external desires. When you use material possessions or accomplish-

> THE LONGING FOR ANYTHING OUTSIDE OF SELF IS A LONGING FOR *SOURCE*.

ments as a means of security, happiness, or fulfillment, you inevitably continue the perpetual cycle of surviving. Advanced levels of surviving is masked as thriving, making it almost impossible to remember.

None of the superficial measures are real. They are constructs that you cannot seem to break away from without feeling like a failure. Then you conceive babies  and teach them all you know. "Abide by my constructs. Make me proud! Go to this college and pursue that career." The cycle only perpetuates, and the curses preserve. So success is not without addiction, depression, oppression, abuse, rape, child molestation, greed, or any other power struggle because the curse has not been transcended. Thus, generations after generations will incarnate with this alternative reality to deal with no matter their accomplishments.

Children are not opportunities to live vicariously. If anything, the core parental purpose is to remove the veil and help your little one remember why they incarnated. Children come equipped to function at the vibration and consciousness of the world they enter. Most often, elders are forcing outdated beliefs on small yet elevated beings.

Elders can guide children while creating safe spaces and opportunities to explore their innate gifts, talents, and interests. It is a more natural undertaking when you allow your inner child to tap into the innate gifts and talents you may have buried to conform. The parts of Self you have not accepted, yet they remain as the avid thoughts and ideas that wake you out of your sleep or the injustices that bring you rage. The rejected parts of Self prompt you to stand in the very question, Who Am I?

This question is only answered when someone chooses to take the journey of the soul. Until someone chooses to create their own benchmarks, sit in darkness for a while, or run the risk of not accomplishing according to society. The challenge is to consider what you truly desire by looking at what it is in your heart that keeps calling you. The question then becomes not so much Who am I? But more so, How much of God's love am I willing to receive? And am I ready to walk inside of love and let it become my soul purpose?

CHAPTER

CHOICE

"NOTHING YOU EXPERIENCE IS CAUSED BY ANYTHING OUTSIDE OF YOU. YOU EXPERIENCE ONLY THE EFFECTS OF YOUR OWN CHOICE."

THE WAY OF MASTERY, LESSON 1

CHOICE

The English language can be a double-edged sword. In this case, we have been conditioned to decide, weigh our options, and eventually kill off, as the suffix -ide denotes one or more options based on perceived circumstances. We are left with one option and a belief that the other options cannot co-exist. Alternatively, choice is underutilized freedom granted to us. The power of choice is our free will. It does not always need to be a well-thought-out, intellectual, or even logical undertaking. It is, after all things considered, choosing from your heart, your gut, the seat of your soul.

> **CHOICE IS UNDERUTILIZED FREEDOM GRANTED TO US.**

Nothing you experience is caused by anything outside of you. To be present in this physical body at this particular time is a choice. The freedom to design your life is the ultimate manifestation of choice. You experience only the effects of your own choice or lack thereof. When you are reactive, blaming others, and deciding that you are stuck in a condition or emotion caused by someone or something else, you are giving away your power. Power, not in the sense of controlling, manipulating, or forcing. Power, in the function of life force, chi, energy, alacrity, aliveness, and wellness.

Every choice you have ever made or have not made leaves you where you are today. Every choice is an experience or a lesson. There is no right or wrong. There is just choice.

Only when we become responsible about our power to choose do we thrive. We thrive once we design a life led by our internal compass. So when choosing, we must also accept the immense responsibility that comes along with choice. There is no one to blame or hide behind in the game of choice.

Consider your life—your parents, the environment you grew up in, your gender, race, socioeconomic background, triumphs, and tragedies—all deliberate choices to give you the experience your soul needs to fulfill your earthly mission.

How would your life experience shift if you began to consider that your reality is made up of choices you made while in heaven? Your transition from heaven and your journey through the birth canal caused you to forget. Your soul, your ancestors, and your spirit guides can help you remember if you choose to connect and ask them for their guidance. It is not the nature of our guides to infringe on our power of choice. It becomes your responsibility then to forward the relationship.

If at any juncture you find that a choice you previously made is no longer serving your highest self, take the time to access and choose again.

[JOURNAL ENTRY 004:
I'LL RISE UP]

Nothing is working. I am barely surviving. Some mornings I literally cannot get out of bed. I am consistently late for work, yet I am setting my alarm earlier each day. I need more time to get myself prepared for the day. Some mornings, I wake up feeling as if I fell down a flight of concrete stairs.

Everything hurts.

The room is spinning. I lay there, tears in my eyes, praying for the strength to move. The pain is just enough to lay back down. By the time I muster the power to turn on the teapot and gulp down a shot of apple cider vinegar, I am clear that I am not making it to work on time. Still pretending I do not feel my lymph nodes protruding as I wash my face. Echoing in the confines of my mind was the persistent yet silent thought, "Am I dying?" I drown out my deep thoughts and dark concerns with the belting tunes of 'Rise Up' by Andra Day.

I hummed softly, "I'll rise up. I'll rise like the day. I'll rise up. I'll rise unafraid. I'll rise up. And I'll do it a thousand times again."

I have seen many doctors, but none could figure out the root cause of what was ailing me. During my last visit, they told me, "your white blood cell count is low, you have a fever, so it is evident your body is fighting off some sort of infection. We are just not sure what the infection is. All of your tests are coming back just fine. I'm going to prescribe Naproxen for the pain, and let's monitor." At that moment, I vowed to not see another doctor. For the sake of sanity, I would find other means to heal my body. If another medical professional utters a pain prescription, I would surely lose my mind. I know that I am not making this stuff up.

At this time, I have been experiencing extreme bouts of severe pain, extreme fatigue, breakouts, headaches, nausea, and fevers for about six months. I want to get to the root of the issue. I have no interest in masking the surface level symptoms with synthetic medicine. I do believe the Earth is the producer of any elixir I require. I am primarily plant-based these days, eating fish on rare occasions. I do not drink alcohol anymore. I guess waking up feeling sick made me lose my desire...

'I'll rise up. I'll rise like the day.'

My physical condition is taking a toll on my mental and emotional health. Choosing to be or feel any other way seems futile. Isolation felt safe but perhaps not healthy. I opted out of a girls' trip to Miami. I love Miami girls' trips, but I could not count on myself to make it through the weekend without a flare-up, so I stayed home. I was hitting a wall, wondering if all this pain was a physical manifestation of the chaos in my mind.

The gravity of 'I Surrender All' was upon me. There was no longer a need or desire to resist. At this point, I directed my energy away from fighting or resisting. I began to trust that my symptoms were not who I was; instead, they were communicating with me. I traded I am sick with I am healing. The reality was something is attacking my body. The truth was I am alive, and as long as I am alive, I will speak life over myself. I am fully aware the body and mind are temporary teaching devices utilized by God's direction. My prayer to God is to guide my steps. My question, "What must I do to restore health in my physical body?" reflected my commitment that there was no stone that I was unwilling to overturn. Ultimately, there is no food, person, place, or thing I am reluctant to part ways with if it interferes with my ultimate intention.

"I'll rise up. I'll rise like the day. I'll rise up. I'll rise unafraid. I'll rise up. And I'll do it a thousand times again."

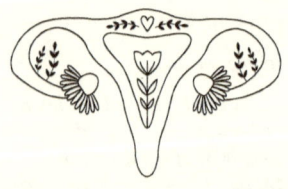

CHAPTER 10

HEALING DIS-EASE

> "ANYTHING THAT ARISES THAT CANNOT PASS THROUGH YOU, THROUGH YOUR UNWILLINGNESS TO EMBRACE IT WITH LOVE, TO FEEL IT COMPLETELY WILL CAUSE 'INDIGESTION' OF THE PHYSICAL, EMOTIONAL, MENTAL AND CAUSAL BEINGS OR BODIES. NOW IMAGINE THE PAIN THAT MANIFESTS IN YOUR PHYSICAL BODY, EMOTIONAL AND MENTAL BODIES WHEN THERE'S A PART OF YOU, AN EXPERIENCE THAT YOU ARE UNABLE TO DIGEST."

THE WAY OF KNOWING, LESSON 27

By now, you have come to discern that you are not just a physical body. You are an intricate weaving of subtle bodies— including the etheric, mental, emotional, astral, and causal. When you experience dis-ease in the physical body, it is often the materialization of what first began in the subtle bodies. Emotions and thoughts are energy when unresolved or unexpressed they become stuck in the body causing energetic blockages. These blockages will eventually register in the physical body as illness.

Any sort of dis-ease of the mind or body is dissonance on a cellular level. It could be an ancestral or karmic resonance registered decades ago or grief, anger, and disconnection in this lifetime. When illness shows up, there lies a profound and sometimes missed opportunity to go under the veil to discover the root cause, lesson, and light within you that is begging for healing

Our western medicine system is indispensable as it reveals inconsistencies in the body with state of the art technology, emergency life-saving surgeries and procedures, and controlling or treating symptoms. It should be used in addition to other practices that are best suited to identify the root of such ailment. Energy workers, healers, and shamans traditionally can assist with identifying and clearing energetic blockages through subtle modalities like reiki, acupuncture, and plant medicine. Well trained Babalawo's and priests can inquire into spiritual and ancestral trauma and blockages that may be taunting you in the physical. Applying these methods and modalities is the all-encompassing integrative self-care that we must move toward if there is an interest in genuinely healing dis-ease, not merely subduing symptoms.

In Barbara Ann Brennan's book *Hands of Light*, she explains, "illness is the result of imbalance. An imbalance is a result of forgetting who you are. Forgetting who you are creates thoughts and actions that lead to an unhealthy lifestyle and eventually to illness. Illness can thus be understood as a lesson you have given yourself to help remember who you are." There are tons of ways to cause an imbalance in the body—environment, diet, exhaustion, depression of the immune systems, overuse of the nervous system, deep-seated emotional pain and trauma.

Healing dis-ease is a journey of choosing to remember, acknowledge, and forgive everyone for everything. The challenge is to be willing to release whatever is obstructing us by assuming responsibility for the choices that created our environment and our reality in this moment.

Any sort of illness is direct communication from the soul and often a sign of spiritual opportunity if you are willing to accept and surrender to what this dis-ease is communicating. For me, it was Lyme disease, chronic fatigue syndrome, and anxiety. For others, it may be depression, asthma, chronic sinus infections, chronic bacterial vaginosis, fibroids, Chron's disease, lupus, fibromyalgia, autoimmune disease, or cancer. There is no limit to the ways illness and dis-ease may register in your particular body. However it may register, understand that it is more of an opportunity than anything.

JOURNAL ENTRY 006
REPRESENTATION IS SPIRITUAL

I am witnessing a mystifying aura about my life. The people, instances, and experiences are showing up at the perfect moment. It all feels supernatural. I recently began assisting as a recorder at a twelve-week seminar on integrity. On the first day, the program leader asked me to identify an area of my life where there was a lack of integrity and the actions I would take during the seminar to restore integrity. I shared with him about my health and the frustration I had been experiencing around it. He looked at me, unshaken, and said, "I got it, let's set a date or a time frame by which your health will be restored." It was as if he had no doubt there was a solution, and I was the problem solver.

I intended to uncover the root cause of what was ailing me and do what was necessary to heal my body. I did not know how or what would possibly shift. Still, I am beginning to understand the power of my word. My word, backed by the sincerity of my intention and the profound listening of community, anything is possible.

Less than six-weeks into the integrity seminar I found myself online doing some research when I came across a list of holistic practitioners in my area. As I scrolled, the image of one of the physicians jolted me. I was overcome with joy and excitement as I read over the biography and credentials for Dr. Maiysha. She owned and operated an integrative medical practice less than a mile from my apartment. It could have been the sincerity of her smile that made me feel comforted or the whisper from Spirit to contact her office. I knew that she would be a pivotal proponent

of my healing. I crossed my fingers as I called her office, "please let her be taking new patients." I was delighted and relieved to learn there was an immediate appointment available.

Spirit has never misdirected my steps.

My appointment with Dr. Maiysha was a spiritual one. For the first time since I have not been feeling well, I felt heard. She was patient, inquisitive, concerned, and she answered all of my questions. We talked about my symptoms, my career, my life, and my interests. It was kismet to learn that she had been significantly involved in the same seminar program I was assisting. We discovered that we shared some mutual friends. She even knew the program leader that infused within me the audacity to set a date for when I would heal myself. I could hardly believe it!

Dr. Maiysha was pretty confident we could get to the root of what was ailing me. She assured me that together we would restore my health. She requested laboratory tests, asked more questions, and made suggestions. I felt better leaving her office than I had felt in months. I never had a physician treat me with such care and concern. In noticing the synchronicity of our fateful meeting, we both wore hunter green on the day of my visit. I saw the rose quartz crystals in her office, the same quartz I had been wearing around my neck. I knew the encounter was divine. On my way out of the office, I hugged her tightly.

Representation is spiritual, to have a safe space to be cared for and listened to is revolutionary. One thing that I knew for sure as I drove away from her office was that I only want to exist in the places, spaces, and relationships that nourish my soul and nurture my individuality.

I was sitting in my car in the parking lot of my office when I got the call with my results. I was diagnosed with Lyme Disease and Chronic Fatigue Syndrome. Surprisingly, I did not cry. I mostly felt relieved. This diagnosis got to the root of what I was experiencing. A foreign entity had infiltrated my body, and it could be eradicated with the correct tools and resources. There was no discussion of treating the symptoms alone. Dr. Maiysha was just as committed to getting to the root as I was. Lyme Disease is tricky to detect and sometimes even more complicated to treat. She created a robust treatment plan that included an alkaline diet, antibiotics, and a host of herbs and supplements to support my gut health and immune system.

I cannot express enough the importance of being respected and understood by the people enlisted to provide me service and care. I know that when called to be the provider, I will bring an unwavering commitment to excellence, integrity, and compassion. I will always be willing to do the work to find genuinely aligned providers.

My Lyme treatment lasted eight-weeks. At the start of the last week of treatment, a friend invited me to attend a sweat lodge at the Community Land Trust. Once we arrived, an older gentleman proceeded to smudge us with sage. He expressed that we could write down what we intended to release and put the paper in the fire pit to burn at any point in the evening. I knew I wanted to cast any Borrelia strains, the bacteria that cause Lyme disease, from my body. I wrote it on the paper and prayed as I released it all into the fire.

For the rest of that evening, we communed with the earth, sang songs, and shared honestly with each other. I was profusely sweating and eternally grateful. It felt like just the release I

needed. Back at home, I am in the shower doing my round of lathering with my hands. Since learning, I had Lyme disease and never experiencing a tick bite the hypochondriac that lives deep within me checks for ticks every day. On this particular night, I felt a small bump under my right arm near my back. I hopped out of the shower to get a closer look in the mirror. Surely, it was a tick. I reached for a tweezer, pulled the tick out, and dropped it in the toilet.

I wrote an email to Dr. Maiysha on the issue. She, too, found it a bit shocking. She invited me to come to the office. After our conversation, I accepted this as the miraculous occurrence it was, the physical manifestation of an answered prayer in the final week of my treatment. I removed a tick from my body the night of my sincere desire for Lyme disease to be removed from my body. This is symbolism. I had completed this process with Lyme disease.

My biggest lesson was the absolute need to develop a relationship with my body where illness can not fester. The moment something is gone awry, my body and I are in communication. This dis-ease incited a very deliberate journey of the soul. The Lyme was only the physical manifestation of something much deeper and more pressing. Alignment over instant gratification became the mantra after this experience. Remembering who I am and why I am here became the goal. Healing the fragmented parts of self became the work. I returned to my seminar with new ears because integrity had become my compass.

CHAPTER

11 -INTEGRITY-

"AND YOU BEGIN TO BE WILLING TO ALLOW CERTAIN THINGS TO FALL OUT OF YOUR LIFE, EVEN FAMILY AND FRIENDS, TRUSTING THAT BECAUSE OF YOUR DESIRE AND INTENTION, WHAT PASSES OUT OF YOUR LIFE MUST BE OKAY. FOR IT WILL BE REPLACED BY NEW VIBRATIONAL PATTERNS WHICH COME IN THE FORM OF MESSENGERS— EVENTS, PLACES, PERSONS AND THINGS— THAT CAN CARRY YOU ON THE UPWARD SPIRAL OF AWAKENING."

THE WAY OF THE HEART, LESSON 5

Integrity is the state of being willing to unlearn the lessons and let go of the illusions you have acquired in life. When observed objectively, the root of your pain and suffering are these illusions—the breeding ground for the dis-ease that manifests physically, mentally, and emotionally.

Integrity requires the sort of discipline that an artist brings to their art, out of the deep desire and delight to create more beautifully. As we travel the upward spiral of awakening, we must acquire a rigor and discipline that lays a reliable foundation for our existence.

Integrity cannot exist without the deliberate release of the fragmented parts of Self. Who you are on the other side of rebirth cannot flourish without integrity. The contradictions that may seem trivial on the surface, when explored more profoundly do significant damage. An example would be saying yes when everything in you is a resounding no.

> WHO YOU ARE ON THE OTHER SIDE OF REBIRTH CANNOT FLOURISH WITHOUT INTEGRITY.

As you navigate your integrity, observe your emotional, spiritual, mental, and physical bodies. Begin bringing to mind your goals, desires, and commitments. What are the things you have said you would do that you have not done nor have a plan to get done—is it going back to school, losing weight, delving into a new adventure, learning an instrument, language, or exploring happiness?

Whatever comes up, it will benefit you greatly to either fulfill or dissolve these desires to maximize your potential and enhance the way you relate to Self. Otherwise, these promises become fragmented within us. Where have you said yes, when you meant no? Where have you not focused on what would provide you the type of life you desire? Where are you placing blame for how things are, how things were, or how things should be? The answers will reveal the many parts of a fragmented self. Though this only begins to scratch the surface, there are also the promises to call someone back, visit a friend, or purchase a present that you used your word to affirm and did not follow through.

What are you eating that does not fuel your body? What relationships are you in that lack fulfillment? Where do you shrink yourself and dim your light? Where do you consistently feel depleted? What outdated beliefs are you

THE LINEAGE OF LOVE

still holding as truth? In what areas do you believe you are lacking or in need of fixing? Where are you waiting on a savior to fix you or to make things happen for you? Are you aware of the ways you self-sabotage?

Now you are beginning to see the impact of using your word impetuously. You may even start to feel sensations come up as you honestly review the fragmented pieces of Self. As you begin to clear out the excess, you allow for a simpler life—a life where you have grown to experience and honor the real power of your word. In reality, it may look like writing out all of your commitments and creating statements to affirm or dissolve. As an example, you may write that "I have always said I will go back to school. I am choosing to dissolve this desire because it is not a priority for me at this time." This simple practice keeps your word impeccable.

When practicing integrity as a discipline, you begin to create your life with intention, zeal, discernment, and promise. Circumstances and excuses become irrelevant as the relationship with Self evolves. Your evolution emerges as the dominant priority, and using your words to create your reality becomes second nature. Without integrity nothing works.

You must stay postured for a miracle. Everywhere you turn, miracles are happening. The key is to remain in a posture to experience and receive the miracles. A posture of gratitude, wonder, and belief is necessary in this case. Belief in what you ask? If you want to experience miracles, you have to believe in magic. Abracadabra is Hebrew; it translates to I create as I speak. Ponder this:

What miracles am I creating with my words? What miracles am I welcoming with my inquiries? If you already know for sure how it will go, the miraculous will not have much room to WOW you.

[JOURNAL ENTRY# 007: ABRACADABRA]

CHAPTER 12

SOUL TIES

> "THEREFORE, WHEN LOVE LEADS THE WAY, WHEN LOVE IS THE FIELD OF ENERGY THAT YOU ARE ABIDING WITHIN, EVERYWHERE YOU GO, YOU ARE TOUCHING THE UNIVERSE IN A WAY THAT IS MUCH MORE SUBTLE THAN THE CONSCIOUS MIND. AND THE UNIVERSE WILL RESPOND TO YOU, BECAUSE LOVE RESPONDS TO ITSELF LIKE A FLOWER THAT OPENS TO SUNLIGHT."
>
> THE WAY OF KNOWING, LESSON 28

You are made up of energy. Everything you interact with is composed of energy. As you navigate life, you are always receiving, storing, and emitting energy. Your home, tangible objects, clothing, and car hold energy. The water you put in your glass, the food you consume, living or dead, has energy. Everything in our existence is interconnected in an electromagnetic field. Vibration refers to the oscillating movement of atoms caused by energy. All humans, animals, plants, and objects have an energy field that holds their vibrational frequency. Frequency is used to determine vibrational patterns measured in hertz (Hz) and is the rate at which a vibration or oscillation occurs.

As you advance in your development stages, you become aware and responsible for the space you take up energetically and the frequency in which you vibrate. There is an optimum vibrational level for all cells and organs in our bodies. An atom that vibrates faster is considered high vibration, while atoms vibrating at lower rates would be regarded as low vibration. Dis-ease, bacteria, and viruses operate at a lower frequency than the optimal human body. When the body's frequency lowers, it becomes a match for the vibrational frequency of dis-ease.

Substances of higher frequency destroy substances of lower frequency. While there is an optimal frequency of the human body, definite elements can lower or raise the frequency. Eating organic foods and herbs will surely increase the human body's vibrational frequency, while processed foods will decrease frequency. People, stress, and environmental pollutants all affect one's vibrational frequency. The body is continually receiving input through energy vibration.

Teaching yourself to notice when your energy field is contracted will prove to be an invaluable lesson in your life's journey. You attract experiences and relationships that match your frequency. When you are faced with a consistent set of circumstances that prevent your potential from being fully realized, it is merely a reflection of your vibration quality. If you are connected with someone you are dissatisfied with, you must go inward to the thoughts and vibrations that allow you to match these relationships, these jobs, or these particular sets of circumstances. It could be a lesson your soul has been longing for or a hidden thought or belief about what you deserve or your worth.

The path of radical self-honesty presents unending opportunities to raise your vibrational frequency by noticing fearful thoughts and identifying them for what they are. Spending quality time with yourself allows you to recognize the frequency you are operating on without interference. There is no judgment, just observation, and ultimately choice.

You train yourself to become the observer of your thoughts and notice the thoughts that add purpose and value. Also, see the views that contract your energy field, leaving you fearful and lacking trust and confidence. You can continue this practice as you enter spaces and engage with people. Take a moment to notice your energy field and ask yourself, "Am I expanding or contracting in this space?" You can choose the thoughts you give life to. You can also choose to excuse yourself from spaces and people that compromise your energetic frequency.

Choosing to separate yourself from another could prove to be beneficial if your interactions with this person are harmful, violent, or unhealthy to you. Suppose a person is the activator of emotions and lessons that you are not ready or willing to learn; rest assured that removing this person will temporarily assuage this discomfort. Still, you will be met with the same set of circumstances, with a different individual, until you choose to heal the parts of Self that are begging to be acknowledged. The resolution of this trigger allows your energetic frequency to rise, not solely removing the individual.

Have you ever noticed someone so full of life and love and how things seem to just work out for them? This is due to an expansive energetic field. When you are reflecting love, people respond to you with kindness and love. You gain the most generous support from the universe, and things work out in your favor because you genuinely believe they will. In this energy field of love, you know you are deserving, and you are confident enough to walk inside the truth of who you are.

As you continue to do the internal work and strengthen your ability to choose the thoughts that influence your life, you become firm in selecting the people and environments that positively complement your experience. You notice low vibrations from afar, and because of the love you have for yourself, you begin to set boundaries to honor the radical self-honesty and peace that is your birthright.

Often when you do the inner work of raising your vibration, whatever is not a match for your elevated frequency will naturally dissolve. Wherever you find yourself deeply attached to a relationship, space, or place, feeling as if you cannot imagine your life without it, you can consider it a soul tie.

Soul ties bring an uncanny familiarity. There is a reassuring feeling of having known each other long before your physical meeting. The way you entered each other's lives may be fated. There is no denying the depth of your connection. Soul ties enhance your experience and forward your earthly mission. These relationships fulfill something on a spiritual level. You know your life is better because of this fateful meeting, and you honor the relationship as such.

When you become attached or resistant to your soul ties, the relationship can trigger just the opposite, thus becoming unhealthy. It triggers ill feelings, thoughts, and emotions. There is an overtone or undertone of a power struggle in the relationship, and you notice that you are obsessing. Strands of possessiveness, jealousy, neediness, codependency, low self-worth, social anxiety, and extreme empathic overload are ever-present.

Developing the characteristics you crave from your soul tie will always prove beneficial for your wellness and autonomy. It takes the keen listening and care of a trained professional—a therapist or energy worker—to help you unbound the cords of attachment. With a professional's assistance, you hone the tools to develop healthy boundaries. You will also begin to understand the dynamics of entanglement, enmeshment, soul ties, karmic relationships, and codependency. These are trauma responses that were learned in childhood or acquired through epigenetics. Despite that, the work is yours to do if you aspire to have healthy, flourishing, and reciprocal relationships.

It seems that the person on the other end of a soul tie attachment manages always to be toxic. Even so, a toxic person does not exist in reality. You will find in time that whatever you are pushing up against in another has little to do with the other person. Sure enough, they are working through their challenges as you are. The desire to change someone, argue or talk through their challenges in hopes that they become someone who makes you more comfortable is a fool's game. It does everyone a disservice when you ignore all the warning signs because they only become more pronounced over time. Essentially, to love another is to accept them how they are. To love oneself is to choose the ones you will co-exist with this lifetime and nurture those relationships accordingly.

True love, bell hooks shared in *All About Love,* "is a

peculiar kind of insight through which we see the wholeness of a person—while accepting the level on which he now expresses himself or herself. There is no delusion that the potential is a present reality. True love requires intention and action. True love accepts the person without qualifications, but with a sincere and unwavering commitment to helping him/her achieve the goals of self-unfoldment—which we may see better than they do."

Soul ties are ultimately lessons guiding you toward self-unfoldment. There is an intricate connection between yourself and the souls you encounter.

As you do the internal work to raise your vibration, the quality of the souls you encounter will enhance, as will your interactions with these souls.

My relationship with you is essentially my relationship with myself. You and I are two souls incarnated on purpose. We both have traumas, karmic debts, and scores to settle in this lifetime. We came to this plane as two completely separate beings, yet we are one... Your very presence in my life is proof of divine order and divine grace. I marvel at the ways we find each other in different forms lifetime after lifetime.

As we navigate this journey, I am here for you and even more so I am here for me. Taking care of you will come naturally to me, I promise to take care of myself. Please promise to take care of yourself. We will be better together because of it.

[JOURNAL ENTRY 008: MIRRORS]

CHAPTER

13 —COMMITMENT—

"THIS REQUIRES A TURNING POINT IN THE SEAT OF THE SOUL, A CHANGING OF THE MOMENTUM OF CONSCIOUSNESS— NOT OUTWARD, BUT INWARD. THIS IS NOT AN ESCAPE FROM THE WORLD— IT IS NOT SOMETHING YOU HAVE TO DO ALL DAY, EVERY DAY. BUT YOU SPEND TIME IN PRAYER AND MEDITATION, FORGIVENESS, BREATHING, AND RELAXING."

THE WAY OF TRANSFORMATION, LESSON 17

THE LINEAGE OF LOVE

Commitment is where you begin to assume full responsibility. Without commitment, who you might be never quite gets off the ground. There must be a commitment to a deep dive inward to experience the fullness of your being. You spend more time becoming self-observant and less time being concerned with what is going on in the world. You adopt a spiritual practice and move further away from the illusions you have created and believe to be your truth. You spend no time blaming the world for your state of being—not parents, society, God, the environment, the Government, nor your astrological chart.

You take full responsibility for what you think, feel, believe, and experience. Assuming full responsibility is not a burden for you to bear but rather an acceptance of power for you to embrace. It is the acceptance that what you are seeking exists within you. Nothing outside of you can truly fulfill you, nor will it fix what you perceive broken. What validates you ultimately must come forth from within you.

Every experience—the good, the bad, and the ugly: the divorce, the abuse, the rape, the molestation, the death, the abortion, the infertility, the betrayal, the career path, the religious doctrine, the car accident, the psychosis, the lawsuit, the infidelity, the depression, and the sexual orientation— all contribute to what you incarnated to do, to be, to create and to complete. It was a choice your soul agreed to experience.

Knowing this does not pacify the reality, nor does it invalidate the overwhelming physical and emotional reaction these experiences trigger. No one gets off the hook, and no wrongs are made right by accepting what appeared to be a very harsh reality as a choice on the path. It does not make any misfortune your fault.

Accepting the parts of self and the experiences that feel indigestible is a necessary step to reclaim your power. Judging yourself or being unreasonably unforgiving to yourself makes it impossible to realize the depth or fullness of your being. Thus, the unrealized fullness of your being inhibits you from realizing the fullness of any being because any relationship you find yourself in is only an extension of the relationship you have with yourself.

Take as many moments as you need to forgive yourself for all things continuously. Otherwise, you will find your load too heavy to soar to greater heights and your reality a mundane repetition of victimization.

Assuming responsibility matures into forgiving everyone so that you take back your power. Grounded in that power, you remember that all events are neutral, and no one did anything to you. According to *The Way of Mastery*, the soul that is genuinely committed to awakening does not flee uncomfortable situations until it believes it has fully extracted all of its wisdom.

You realize it is time to be with who you are with—or the ones you are with— the patterns that play out in these relationships are essentially the patterns that have become dogma, the lens from which you view your world. We can then look upon our mates, our lovers, our family, and our world as entirely innocent.

During these moments of introspection, it is worthwhile to ask yourself the following questions: what is my typical complaint? Why do I desire to attract these experiences? What is the lesson my soul is begging to learn? Allow these answers to come to you.

When you commit to accepting full responsibility for your life, you will quickly find that you cannot be victimized. The work may start with looking to your parents and forgiving them for how you perceived they had failed you. The work may continue with forgiving past lovers and friends. However, the work will mature with forgiving yourself for the perceptions and assumptions you have made in error.

Forgiving creates so much space. Space to feel something new, freedom to create new experiences, and freedom to relate to yourself, family, friends, and community in new and profound ways. To forgive does not mean you let someone off the hook. Nor does it mean you veer from the reality that a grievance has occurred. To forgive is not something to offer to another as a submission or a great act of strength or morality. Forgiving accepts what happened and allows you to acknowledge and release the valid feelings and emotions that sprouted from this infraction.

Each time we forgive ourselves or another, we take ourselves in the depth of our own consciousness's purity. Forgiveness is an essential key to evolution. It frees you from guilt, shame, shock, projection, and separation. Alternatively, you continue to suffer terribly, often creating false self-images that portray you as 'the victim' or the 'good/righ-

> **WHEN YOU CHOOSE TO FORGIVE INTENTIONALLY, YOUR CAPACITY TO LOVE GROWS DEEPER.**

teous' person when the reality is you are neither.

When you choose to forgive intentionally, your capacity to love grows deeper. Love is the change agent. "Love" as James Baldwin poetically portrayed in *The Fire Next Time*, "takes off the mask that we fear we cannot live without and know we cannot live within." Baldwin uses the word '*love*,' "not merely in the personal sense but as a state of being, or a state of grace—not in the infantile American sense of being made happy but in the tough and universal sense of quest, daring, and growth."

What you refuse to forgive in the world is what you also refuse to forgive in yourself. There is no separation. Though we often choose to live in the illusion that we are separate beings on separate paths. We are not. The emotions you refuse to release will create a vulnerability in your body, allowing your organs to be a viable host for dis-ease.

Commitment is doing the work until you can state the facts without assumption and choose after all things considered; This is fertile ground for healing. In the process, you become the healer fully equipped to heal yourself. There are no quick fixes. Nothing will evolve without your full commitment and sincere intention. You may seek assistance and rely on many tools, though the crux of the work cannot be outsourced.

[JOURNAL ENTRY #009: 21 DAYS OF FORGIVENESS]

Today I felt lonely; I cried so hard my head was beginning to spin. Feelings of anger were ever present, and I needed physical touch like a lifeline. My hips were so tight. I just wanted to be held; I thumbed through my journal to find an empty page and landed on this:

"It's going to get uncomfortable. There will be uncertainty. You got this. Don't doubt what you know to be because it seems unachievable or because you are uncertain. In a moment of uncertainty—pray, meditate, get on your yoga mat, read this! Just don't fret, don't deny, don't doubt. You. Got. This. You were made for this. You are powerful beyond measure."

So I got on the mat, my practice was going perfect, and then there was half-pigeon pose. As I inhaled, I felt the tears rushing. I closed my eyes as if to turn off the faucet. Suddenly, a thought came to me: "How is it possible to truly love or extend grace to another without grace and unconditional love for self?"

At that moment, the yoga instructor placed her hands on my lower back, assisting as I eased deeper into the pose. My thoughts continued, "What if you were boldly yourself at any given moment?" "What if anger were okay for you to express and okay in others?" I surrendered into the pose, deeper into the tightness I felt in my hips and deeper into the anger, the sadness, the guilt, and the grief that overcame me. The tears flowed freely. I surrendered to the moment and left the class feeling lighter, softer, and more forgiving. I needed that.

As I relaxed into my evening at home, I perused my bookshelf for a new read. A few years ago, my sister, Leah, went to Oprah's Super Soul Sessions, where she purchased Iyanla Vanzant's book, 21 Days of Forgiveness. The book guides the reader through twenty-one days of forgiving yourself, the people in your life, and the world for everything. The premise is to release the burdens of the past using forgiveness as a path to freedom. The process was a series of meditations, clearly defined writing prompts, and the use of Emotional Frequency Tapping (EFT), a tool used to release stagnant energy and trapped emotions. EFT is a concept rooted in traditional Chinese medicine. You gently tap on meridian points in your body while focusing on a particular statement to help move out blocked energy. The practice is similar to acupuncture without the use of needles.

It was my first time practicing tapping. I learned that some of this practice's therapeutic effects commonly benefit those dealing with anxiety, post-traumatic stress disorder, weight loss issues, stress, and several other conditions. For 21 Days, I am committed to tapping myself to complete forgiveness. I started a new journal to detail my experience and also to write out my forgiveness statements.

The work uncovered during 21 Days of Forgiveness was mindblowing. It is no wonder my hips were so tight. I was holding a lot. As I am writing my forgiveness statements, I immediately realize that I had feelings of anger, frustration, and disgust toward men. "April 24th. Day 13. I forgive men. I forgive the men that hurt my sisters, my girlfriends, my aunts, my cousins, my mother, me. I forgive them, and I set them free." Only a few days later, and my notes on men are now tear-streaked as I allow myself to forgive a world that did not feel like home to me for so long. Then there were the remnants of injustices that formed knots in my shoulders. I am still feeling the pain from the 1999 shooting of Amadou Diallo, a 23-year-old native of Guinea, furthering his education in New York City. He reached for his wallet to present identification, and the NYPD shot forty-one times, killing him. His experience, the news stories, the not guilty verdict lived so profoundly within my cells. Just the thought produced such pain, anger, and hopelessness.

I desire to breathe deeper, to experience the fullness of every moment.

Forgiveness had become the gateway.

I choose to forgive everyone for everything.

Not for them, for me.

PART III

CHAPTER 14

GOLDEN JOURNEY

"THEN, THERE WAS A MOMENT FOR EACH AND EVERY ONE OF YOU WHEN THE DECISION WAS MADE WITHIN YOUR CONSCIOUSNESS, WITHIN YOUR MIND, THAT CONDITIONS WERE APPROPRIATE FOR YOU TO AGAIN INCARNATE. THERE ARE MANY, MANY FACTORS THAT ATTRACT THE SOUL TO YET AGAIN CONDENSE INTO PHYSICAL FORM. BUT THE CHIEF AMONG THESE IS THE PERCEPTION AND THOUGHT THAT THERE IS YET SOMETHING LEFT UNDONE. THERE IS YET SOME LESSON THAT CANNOT BE REALIZED SAVE WITHIN THE PHYSICAL DOMAIN. THERE IS INDEED A PURPOSE THAT YOU, AS A SOUL, WOULD YET WISH TO FULFILL.

THE WAY OF TRANSFORMATION, LESSON 17

THE LINEAGE OF LOVE

There comes a time in human existence when we experience our version of the crucifixion. It is what we have come to know as ego death. Ego death is a complete loss of subjective self identity. You begin questioning your very existence. Nothing seems to be working out in the way that you anticipated. All of your efforts appear to be in vain. You are in the space between who you were and who you will become. Many refer to this space as the Dark Knight of the Soul.

An ego death may be ushered in by an external trigger, event, or disaster. It could be the sudden loss of a close family member or friend, for example. An illness or natural disaster, terrorist attack, or global pandemic. A major life transition—marriage, divorce, relocation, or a pregnancy. Another major trigger is when Saturn, the planet of upheaval and discipline, returns to the sign it was in on the day you were born. Astrologists call this your Saturn return which happens roughly every 28 to 30 years. Everything that gives meaning to your life—most notably, the illusions begins to collapse, leaving you bare and malleable.

Your soul awakens to its rightful place as the authority, yet your ego has no interest in relinquishing control. The deeply tumultuous internal battle can manifest itself as significant pain, depression, and confusion. This current state can last intermittently for the rest of your life or until you surrender to the golden journey.

The golden journey is when *love* returns to the place of authority. During this journey, careers will change, the quality of your relationships will shift for the very meaning and purpose of existence has evolved. You are awakening to something different, not based on your mind or the illusions that have been impressed on you since birth. The things used to fill your voids are now meaningless.

What makes the journey golden is your willingness to grow through the cycle presented. The Japanese have an art form called 'Kintsukuroi,' which translates to "golden repair." The kintsukuroi or kintsugi (golden joinery) process uses gold to mend back together pieces of broken pottery. As a philosophy, the breakage and repair become incorporated in the object, resulting in a beautiful piece of art instead of many fragments that you must discard. This art form is quite the depiction of life, as outdated parts of you shatter, and while breakage feels inevitable, there is no part of your journey that you ought to discard. All the elements of you congeal to unveil resilience, grit, and ultimate beauty.

There is blissful freedom available to you as you journey. You may come close to this freedom and find it uncomfortable, unlike anything you have experienced, so you run away. You will only run to another form of energy, a web of relationships, or a set of circumstances that force you to stay with what is uncomfortable until you surrender to your spiritual awakening.

Gratefully, this journey of the soul is not a new concept. There are ancient tools and resources to assist as you navigate. Depending on the date, time, and region you were born, you have a detailed depiction of where every planetary coordinate was when you took your first breath; it is called a natal chart. These placements, aspects, and numbers can give you an enormous amount of transformational insight into who you are— your personality traits and predispositions, what you are here to do, experience, and accomplish. Your natal chart can even detail some of the challenges you may encounter along the way.

Pre-colonialism, it was tradition for parents to take their newborn babies to a trusted Ifa Priest or village elder for divination. This ancient science allows for communication between Self, God, and the ancestors. While astrology and numerology offer invaluable insight, divination provides clarity, precise wisdom, and solutions to the questions and concerns that may arise during your life cycle. Ifa divination does not fortune-tell; Ifa divination moves you toward liberation. It will not just gather information, it will assess a spiritual investigation into what needs to be done on earth and in heaven to avoid self-destructive behavior and fulfill your destiny.

The Dagara people of West Africa would say that "children do not belong completely to the parents who gave them birth. They have used their parents' bodies to come through, but they belong to the community and to the spirit." Sobunfu Some shared in her book *The Spirit of Intimacy*, "when a woman is pregnant, a hearing ritual is performed." During such a ritual, questions are asked of the unborn child and based on responses channeled through the mother's voice, the elders will begin to prepare for the baby. "After the birth, the elders make sure they surround the child with things that will help her remember and accomplish her purpose in life."

It is a colonial and non-traditional phenomenon to walk the earth so disconnected from *Source*, separated from community, and without the necessary tools of remembrance. You will notice these tools of remembrance, like divination, have been deemed demonic. Like any sacred text, the Holy Bible has unfortunately been misused by many to suppress your ancient spiritual practices in the guise of God's will.

The banishment of traditionalism has left generations of humans wholly dissociated from their spirituality. You are awakening. Consequently, you must be vigilant to the war for your soul; it can be subtle and disguised when unconscious, yet no less malevolent. Connection to your ancient lineage is where your power lies. It is nearly impossible to control a person who knows who they are and what they are capable of. It is no wonder they vilify the very gifts, abilities, and resources meant to set you free. There is a deep and utter dependence on the ego to remain pacified by illusion.

> **CONNECTION TO YOUR ANCIENT LINEAGE IS WHERE YOUR POWER LIES.**

The golden journey is your commitment to getting to the core of who you are and adopting the practices that will embrace your quest for self-discovery, not suppress it.

CHAPTER 15

THE PORTAL OF INITIATION

"IT IS ALWAYS WHEN YOU ARE AT THE POINT OF YOUR GREATEST SENSE OF DARKNESS, OR YOUR GREATEST FEELING THAT THE LIGHT JUST CANNOT QUITE GET INTO YOU, THAT YOU COULD NOT POSSIBLY EVER BE ENLIGHTENED—IT IS AT THAT MOMENT THAT YOU NEED ONLY INVITE THE LIGHT. AND THE LIGHT BEGINS TO TRANSFORM THE DARKNESS. IT IS WHEN YOU ARE AT YOUR EDGE OF DARKNESS THAT THE DAWN IS BUT A BREATH AWAY...IF YOU WILL BUT STEP FORWARD, THE WHOLE POWER OF THE LINEAGE WILL SUPPORT YOU."

THE WAY OF KNOWING, LESSON 34

THE LINEAGE OF LOVE

Initiation is the beginning of something. We experience many initiations throughout life, birth being the inaugural and death being the final. Our soul holds memories of sacred initiations that preceded birth and even those to come. As you pass through your particular portal of initiation, be it spiritual, physical, emotional, or mental, know that your destiny is heavily supported. The veil between the spirit realm and the living is thin. Your access to ancient wisdom and spiritual guidance is without interference.

The pathways to initiation are copious. *The Way of Mastery* is a pathway to initiation. Cultivating the keys to the kingdom, dismantling illusion, coming into remembrance, forgiving, healing, and learning to love without condition are the principles that facilitated me through this particular portal of initiation. The culmination of initiation enables you, the initiate, to live according to your truth. According to the strand of your lineage expressed through you. Upon taking full responsibility for your life and the experiences that make up your life, you have the unique opportunity to reach complete transfiguration in your human consciousness. You no longer walk this planet in a dormant state.

THE PORTAL OF INITIATION

At the culmination of *The Way of Mastery*, Lesson 34 shared the story of Jesus through the lens of the messiahship. Jesus, a strand of light expressing itself through the tradition of the Jewish family. Like Jesus, all souls have their lineage. "There are strands expressed through India. There are strands expressed through Tibet. Some strands or lineages extend themselves through the South Americas. Some strands or lineages have extended themselves through the North American Indians." 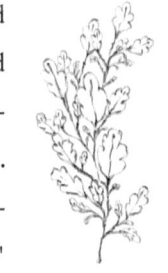 Though I resonated with many of these strands, I intuitively knew that a strand expressed through me was not articulated here. "What is the strand that would propel me through transfiguration?" For a few days, I meditated on this question.

Seemingly unrelated, I was hitting a wall at my job and in the constant inquiry of what is next. A dear friend introduced me to her Godfather, a trusted Babalawo. She recommended that I consult the oracle of Ifa. I have had readings done in the past— astrology, numerology, tarot, and intuitive readings— but I had never had an Ifa divination that peered into my destiny, recollecting what I prayed for while in heaven. Though the concept of Ifa was new to me, it was absolutely what my soul had been in an adamant search for.

It was a Sunday afternoon in late September, the sun was beaming through my bedroom windows, and I was basking in the rare occasion of rest. Laying in bed, journaling insights from my dream, the vibration from my phone interrupted my thought. The Babalawo was calling me back from Lagos to share his insight on the divination.

To my surprise, I received little direction on the job. The messages that resonated most deeply with me were about my health—the divination spoke of an illness and what I would need to do to overcome it. It also spoke of the nightmares I have been having. Finally, the Babalawo said that full Ifa initiation was imminent, it would save my life. I did not clearly understand what this meant, but it resonated so deeply with my soul that it felt like the resounding truth. I asked many questions; as I gained clarity, I was confident that this conversation was the answer to the question I had been meditating on "What is the strand

---

"WHAT IS THE STRAND THAT WOULD PROPEL ME THROUGH TRANSFIGURATION?"

THE PORTAL OF INITIATION

that would propel me through transfiguration?"

While the physical words and lessons in *The Way of Mastery* were coming to a culmination, a new phase of life was beginning. The strand that expressed itself through me was the strand of Yoruba tradition. I traveled to Lagos, Nigeria, to fulfill the promises I made while in heaven. Ifalomo, 'The Child of Ifa' is the Yoruba name I was given, it is the essence of my higher self. My heavenly host revealed this path to me in response to my sincerest desires and most pressing questions. I was born to praise the Orisa.

Time and space are two grand illusions. When you are ready to take your rightful place on Earth, you are entering the ultimate portal of initiation. This is the portal that takes you through life. There will be a need to reinitiate along the way as you take up your proper place on Earth by choosing to remember the truth about how extraordinary you are. You are standing at the edge of the portal of initiation. The choice is always yours to walk through or to turn back. If you turn back from the portal, you remain in a perpetual cycle of fighting for life, always in search of something to make you feel alive.

Life force energy keeps us alive in our present bodies. Many ancient cultures define the concept of life force us-

THE LINEAGE OF LOVE

ing various languages. In India—or yoga class, it is called Prana. In the Chinese language, it's chi. Both terms translate to 'breath.' In Yoruba, it is asé. Chi differentiates a corpse from a living human being. The concept of life force is breath. Low chi makes us physically fatigued and prone to dis-ease. There is not much energy to do more than remaining physically alive, surviving. On the other hand, strong chi is a vibrancy and vitality that enables you to live in the fullness of life, creating, attracting, and manifesting as you flow.

Wherever you find yourself on the journey, know that you are a spiritual being having a human experience. Nothing is done by mistake or without purpose. It is your birthright to live in abundance and to remember why you chose to be on Earth. The choice is yours at any point to say yes to your transfiguration. Your journey may take weeks, years, or many lifetimes before you step into your truth. If you choose to walk through the portal of initiation, you will begin to experience life as a force; this is what it means to be alive.

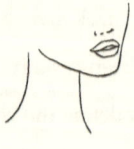

Do you trust yourself enough to do it?

That is ultimately what you are faced with.

There are no external circumstances, those are illusions.

The concerns that spill through, soiling the dream—Those are illusions too.

What you stand up against, is yourself.

You already know that it's all alchemy.

You already know that the universe will conspire.

You know your gifts.

You have the passion—You have the will, the grit.

You will never come to know the answer to this question: Am I truly capable?—

From a place of wonder.

You actually have to do it to find out.

Go get what's yours.

[JOURNAL ENTRY #010:
11:11]

CHAPTER 16

YOUR EDGE

> "IF YOU ARE FEELING EMOTIONS, IF YOU ARE FEELING LIKE YOU WANT TO RUN, IF YOU FEEL LIKE YOU WANT TO AVOID TAKING RESPONSIBILITY FOR SOMETHING THAT HAS BEEN DROPPED IN YOUR LAP, REST ASSURED, RIGHT THERE IS YOUR EDGE. THERE IS YOUR PLACE YOU NEED TO TURN BACK AND EMBRACE."

THE WAY OF KNOWING, LESSON 26

If you have created anything in this lifetime, you likely had a moment when you considered giving up. Maybe what you were working towards did not seem worth the frustration, or in an instance, you felt incapable of going on. I witness this often as a birth doula, there at the cusp of bringing in new life, the birthing person reaches active labor. Perhaps she is walking, rocking, or humming. She has created a ritual of breathing through contractions as they come, and in between contractions, she is resting. I see her close her eyes to nap, sip a smoothie, or chew on ice chips. Things seem calm and manageable. As she moves to the transition stage, there is a shift in her energy. With a keen eye, you may notice beads of sweat forming; this is typically where she begins to vocally deny her ability to bring forth this life, "I can't do it, I'm tired." At this point, the baby is closest to this side; the head may even be crowning. This point of transition is her edge; the only work left is to surrender because the birth of a new soul is imminent.

The edge is where the transformation happens. You have accelerated to the highest point of being in this particular state; your *Spirit* guides can communicate with you without interruption. Here is where you discover and

THE LINEAGE OF LOVE

accept supernatural gifts. The gifts of spiritual communication include—clairvoyance, clairaudience, astral travel, sharing with souls that have departed the earthly realm, and the ability to see and read another's soul. These are the gifts we begin to accept and operate from on the other side of ego death.

At your edge, you sit with your feelings and allow them to direct you. You are allowing your anger to show you where you feel hopeless. Your fear shows you what you care about deeply. Your anxiety or depression helps you reveal the imbalance in your life. At the edge, you do not deny these emotions. You become curiously engaged with whatever shows up, understanding that these emotions are temporarily passing through, with communication for you. No matter how uncomfortable it feels, you name, accept and willingly dissolve whatever shows up.

Have you ever been happy, so filled with joy, that you choose to watch a sad movie or do something to make yourself feel angry because you feel uncomfortable being so happy? How preposterous, right? Yet, we do this to placate the emotions and feelings that we decided were intolerable. Oh, I'm feeling sad; let me watch a funny movie or have a glass of wine to alleviate this uncomfortable emotion.

When, in fact, allowing that emotion to pass through uninterrupted will be the only action that moves you along.

While at your edge, you must be conscious of the time you spend in your head. In your head, you can replay events thousands of times. You relive traumatic experiences, evaluating the meaning of past conversations or events, ultimately adding meaning and story around a situation not based in reality. As a result, you enter a vortex of painful and unproductive streams of consciousness. Begin a practice where you speak only facts, get into the habit of differentiating your personal truth from the facts. The path that lays before you in this moment is your revolution. Your revolution is a ripe opportunity to stand firm and content as your entire world burns to the ground.

> **THE PATH THAT LAYS BEFORE YOU IN THIS MOMENT IS YOUR REVOLUTION.**

When you are at your edge, you are exactly where you need to be on your journey. Move as slowly as you need, enlist as much assistance as required but keep moving forward. The only way out is through; you have made it this far.

I experience life as an individual and I experience life as the collective. It requires a lot of mindfulness because the weight of the collective can be extremely heavy. Too heavy for any individual to take on. I'm going to go out on a limb and say that anxiety and depression is heavily affecting the collective right now. I feel it. I am experiencing it. And what I've come to find as a remedy is a sage. Your sage may be your mama, your friends mama, your girlfriend, your auntie, your teacher, your therapist. She holds space for you. She's spiritually grounded. She exudes love. She passes no judgment. She gives no advice; instead, she is led by Spirit to offer words and resources that leave you full, heard, loved, and equipped for your battle. She holds your hand be it literally or theoretically. She listens. She's generous with her time, her space, and her wisdom. She's there for you. She's been there before, right where you are. She knows what you are dealing with and her faith allows her to reassure you that it gets better. She speaks over your life and has the vision and foresight to see what's possible for you. Even when you can't see it. You get you a sage. Seek out your sage, share with her what you're dealing with, and watch God in human form wrap the love of the divine feminine around you until you can pick yourself up and walk again. Until you feel lighter. Until you can see clearly. Until you sleep through the night. Until your tears are dry. Until you are at peace in your soul.

*She refers to the divine feminine, in reality, she may be he, him, or they.

[JOURNAL ENTRY #011: SAGE]

CHAPTER 17

TAKE UP YOUR CROWN

"IT IS IN THE CRUMBLING OF STRUCTURES YOU HAVE MADE, WHERE YOU ARE BEST GIVEN THE OPPORTUNITY TO REALIZE THE GREAT POWER WITHIN YOU TO TEACH ONLY LOVE. YET, THE EGO WOULD CONVINCE YOU THAT TO KNOW LOVE, YOU MUST SET UP YOUR WORLD SO THAT YOU NEVER EXPERIENCE THE CHALLENGES AND THE INSECURITIES OF ABANDONMENT, ALONENESS, AND NOT-KNOWINGNESS...THE ATTEMPT TO CREATE MATERIAL SECURITY FLOWS ONLY FROM THE EGOIC MIND. FOR THE ENLIGHTENED MIND IS IN COMPLETE ABUNDANCE, ALWAYS."

THE WAY OF KNOWING, LESSON 32

THE LINEAGE OF LOVE

It is quite true that a person born of love can be misunderstood by the world. Such a person is the essence of wind. You do not know where they have been, nor do you know where they are going, and neither do they.

They listen to the voice of *Spirit*, flowing within the infinitude of creativity. They exude courage. They are leaning into the mysteriousness of their being, and their lives are so unorthodox— this is what it looks like to take up your crown.

You allow yourself to become one with *Source*, turning away from the collective momentarily to focus inward on Self. You begin to resolve why you are here while you cultivate and hone the gifts you bring to the collective.

At the moment you choose to relinquish the dream of the dreamer, when you are no longer seeking something outside of yourself for fulfillment, you are ready to follow the pathway that brings your soul into perfect remembrance.

You are no longer fighting for love. You are not begging for acknowledgment or protesting for justice. Instead, you become aware of your innate power and the force of your lineage. You are allowing yourself to uproot from the very places and systems that refuse to acknowledge the essence of your being.

External elements and internal blockages begin to fall as you mend the breakage within yourself and your lineage. With love, you emerge into the surety of who you are, understanding that everything that transpired up until this point was divine order meant to bring you to this culminating reality.

Choice sets things in motion. Taking up your crown is a choice to be made eternally. Take up your crown in all of the spaces that your best Self is not appreciated, honored, respected, or reciprocated. These are the spaces you have become overly committed to integration, where you squander energy fighting for the bare minimum.

> WITH LOVE, YOU EMERGE INTO THE SURETY OF WHO YOU ARE

The alternative is to remain in a cyclical reality of outrage, pain, and disappointment. The opposing party may give a little to pacify your outcry at the moment. Still, the appeasement is an illusion, merely a false hope when the root of the transgression has not been eradicated. In this cycle, you accept a gift, higher salary, an apology, or perceived justice as an indemnification, but the unadulterated truth is that nothing has changed. Your crown has been misplaced with the potentiality of what could be.

I would liken this cyclical reality to the plight of people of African descent in the United States. In its current historical existence, America has never had a genuine interest in the life, evolution, sustainability, safety, or progress of Black people. It is painful to witness such a distinguished group of beautiful, righteous, overtly genius, creative beings begging to be seen, heard, and treated with bare minimum respect and equality.

America pacified our forefathers with integration; we contend with systems forced to integrate us when there was entirely no interest to do so. Generation after generation, we are reminded of this truth. It is a truth that is immutable; who you and I become and how we choose to navigate this truth is, however, shifting.

Transformation occurs when the individual work begins to benefit the collective, which reprograms generations to come. As you each individually take up your crown, the way you view the world starts to crumble, allowing a new collective reality to emerge.

You venerate your ancestors with the same fervor and sanctity that you revere other deities who have walked the earth just as your foremothers and forefathers have. You pool resources to buy the land because you finally get that no one will give you anything. No politician, no bill, no legislation will ever reinstitute what has been taken or lost in this old paradigm. You begin to accept that ultimately your reparations are in the seeds you sow into the land. You know that you will reap the benefits because complete abundance has always been your birthright.

You start to tap into your own creative and spiritual gifts. You create the businesses, the organizations, and watch over your communities—this is what it looks like to take up your crown. You are coming into alignment, giving up your perceived comfort, your golden coins, trusting that giving up the illusion is what will allow you to reap ten million golden coins.

This pathway requires the cultivation of the keys to the kingdom. Everything begins with a desire. The most essential of these keys is allowance because it requires cultivation in time. When there is a desire for healing and awakening, justice becomes the cry of the soul.

Your Creator, through *Spirit*, is working to reshape every moment of your experience—every single moment is divinely orchestrated. Have you noticed that the proper lessons, books, people, and environments are beginning to show up on your path?

As you take up your crown, know that you are not alone. The lineage backs you, and it is you that must allow

for ongoing support. Find your tribe, those like-minded beings journeying on a similar path; it makes all of the difference. Find a therapist you can trust and allow yourself to work through the trauma, the outdated conversations. Try energy healing, reiki, or begin a practice—yoga, meditation, cycling, running, or qi gong. Learn how to breathe. You may even want to develop a skill—gardening, birth work, plumbing, or contracting.

Essentially, taking up your crown is an opportunity to consciously and intentionally do the soul work that will transform your life and the lives of all those on your path. Your path is connecting to *Source* in a more meaningful way. Leaning on your Ori is the physical manifestation of Proverbs 3:5-6, *"Trust in the Lord with all your heart, and do not depend on your own understanding. Seek his will in all you do, and he will show you which path to take."* (NLT)

CHAPTER 18

OTITO
(TRUTH)

> "SURRENDER ALL THOUGHT OF WHAT YOU KNOW AND HAVE BELIEVED. REST IN GRATITUDE TO THE ONE WHO HAS BIRTHED YOU. ASK ONLY TO BE REVEALED FOR YOUR GREATER TRUTH, GREATER WISDOM, GREATER CAPACITY TO KNOW AND EXTEND PERFECT LOVE, PERFECT TRUST, AND PERFECT PEACE."
>
> THE WAY OF KNOWING, LESSON 35

THE LINEAGE OF LOVE

Otito is the Yoruba word that translates to the concept of truth.

In Ifa, there is a holy odu *'Osa'Tura'* that says, "Speak the truth tell the facts. Those who speak the truth are those whom the *Spirit*s will help." Self-transformation is getting to the truth of who you are sans any assumptions about anything.

> **SPEAK THE TRUTH TELL THE FACTS**

Don Miguel Ruiz wrote a wildly popular book called *The Four Agreements*. In this practical guide to personal freedom, he identified the human tendency to make assumptions as the cause of most suffering and internal conflict. "Find the courage to ask questions and to express what you really want. Communicate with others as clearly as you can to avoid misunderstandings, sadness, and drama. With just this one agreement, you can completely transform your life."

Those who speak the truth are those that the deities will help.

Truth is a universal virtue that many spend lifetimes on a quest for. Truth is in your being. Allow *Self* to be Truth. There is no need to wait for someone to tell you who you

OTITO (TRUTH)

are or what you are supposed to be doing. Trust your soul to direct you to the highest possible path for your mission.

There are so many books and philosophical renderings on the power of thought. As the adage states, "as you think, so shall you be." Our thoughts are rooted so deeply in our conscious and unconscious beliefs before we took our first breath. The truth will assist you in dealing with such hidden thoughts. You will invariably manifest your thoughts. Your chi will flow in the direction of your most persistent thoughts.

Life now requires a new level of centeredness, a sense of peace, and an evolved understanding of knowing. You cannot defy the truth. Once you choose to go through the portal of initiation, the only way out is through. You cannot undo the knowledge of the truth of who you are. You can never deny your birthright, your power, or your anointing on the other side of the portal of initiation. Your mind is already healed. There is no destination to arrive. There is only you operating in the pure grace, love, and joy that birthed you.

So what is the truth?

There is nothing you lack, and nothing on this Earth can add more to you. There is nothing that will diminish your being if it were taken away from you.

The truth is the word that cannot fall because it is rooted and grounded in reality. The truth does not exist in our heads, nor does it exists in our interpretation of an experience. It does not wish something was a certain way or that one will become a certain way. In fact, the truth requires you to surrender all hopes and desires that are not grounded in reality. The truth is coming into alignment. Alignment is the willingness to reckon that you are provided with precisely what you need in each moment.

Root yourself inside of a community that waters the flower that is you. It may be the family you were born into; quite often, it is not. Develop a community of like-minded souls that genuinely works for all members of the community. Root yourselves in *Spirit* and work with the doctrines and rituals that speak to the spirit of your community. Without relying on the spirit of your community, you begin to wither.

Relinquish your attachment to what you were told, to what has been ingrained in you. All events are neutral; it is you who attaches meaning and attributes a label— good or bad, right or wrong, inferior or superior— Who told you what was good or bad? Was it the same system

OTITO (TRUTH)

and structure that taught you that you were inferior? Is it rooted in the same doctrines that were force-fed to your ancestors?

The truth is, the table has already been prepared for you before you incarnated. The question that must be answered within the inner sanctums of yourself: Am I willing to walk in my truth?

Have you suffered enough?

Have you kept yourself small long enough?

Have you tasted limitation deeply enough to know that you want these things no longer?

Would you be willing to patiently choose the dissolving of your illusions?

Are you willing to experience perfect peace and freedom?

How will you honor your ancestors?

What are their names?

What path of initiation is sitting in your heart, calling you home?

[JOURNAL ENTRY #012, REFLECTION]

OUTRO: MODUPE

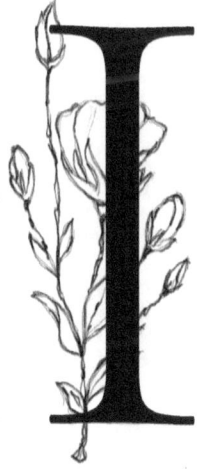

I want to extend my deepest gratitude to you for completing this book. Thank you. Modupe. Thank you for allowing me to share the truth that I have come to know with you. This work is an offering to my lineage, to my *Spirit* allies that show up each time I called out for help, to my family that stood in the gap with me and loved on me through the ebbs and flow of life.

If you have made it to this point of reading these words, I know that you have been on your own golden journey. I hope you know that you are right where you need to be. You are perfect; you are divine, not lacking anything. Earth is the marketplace—continue to shop

> YOU ARE PERFECT; YOU ARE DIVINE, NOT LACKING ANYTHING.

around, explore, experience—all the things, places, spaces, and doctrines that make up Earth. Your truth is so personal, and it is such an individual endeavor. It does not need to be validated. It does not need to look or feel like anyone else's. It just needs to resonate deeply in the center of your being. When you arrive at your center, you will attract like-minded humans to journey with.

I currently reside in Atlanta, Ga., miles away from the family I was born into. Being 'alone' in a city has given me space and opportunity to be one with myself, nurture my relationship to *Spirit*, and the many guides seen and unseen walking with me. The word alone above is in quotations because it is a perception proven to be untrue. I have learned that I am always surrounded by love. Since planting my roots in Georgia, I feel the presence of my ancestors and the strength of my lineage here.

Along this journey, I have had the honorable joy of staying closely connected with my family and community at home while building, developing, and creating family, community, and home wherever I plant myself. The foundation of love, family, and community follow me everywhere I go. It took some time and discomfort for me to remember this. In hindsight, this foundation was ev-

OUTRO: MODUPE

er-present as I matriculated through Howard University. I saw a glimpse of it when I took my first solo trip to Cape Town, South Africa. I was overcome by this love the first time I stood in the labor and delivery room and witnessed a birth as a doula. And now, finally, I've arrived at a place where I accept and desire to be at home wherever I am planted. I have finally understood that there is no such thing as separation.

I have had an intimate connection with the pain of loneliness and equally the beauty of solitude. I have dealt with family trauma that I would not have had access to in the midst of family. Trauma is not limited to what you've experienced or even remember. Undoubtedly, generational trauma, residual habits, and social constructs are passed down in our families through epigenetics. Our families can absorb trauma seven generations from the past and seven generations into the future. For context purposes, the physical, mental, emotional, and spiritual trauma enforced upon those who endured the transatlantic slave trade still ails its descendants and, when left uninterrupted, continues by design. Once the trauma is unveiled, the shapeshifting begins.

You, my dear, are shapeshifting.

There is no blueprint for how your time on Earth will unfold. Your journey equally depends on how much pain you are willing to sit with and how much joy you are willing to be filled with. Free will is an absolute concept. What is for you and what you tangibly have will look massively different solely based on your personal beliefs about what you are worthy of and the choices you make based on these beliefs.

A commitment to live in the vast abundance that your Creator intended for you is needed. This includes genuine humility, not the polite humility you use to shrink yourself or subconsciously bait for more attention inauthentically. Real humility is settling into your pathway to *Source* and co-creating this life experience in all of your power while knowing this life is not your own. There is a force beyond human intellect that allows you to be in existence. There will be a time, unbeknownst to you, where you will cease to be. True humility will enable you to live fully, remove what is in the way, and honor your life with reverence.

The purpose of your creation is to be the Light of God, so you choose to acknowledge that purpose and be the Light of God. May you shine ever so brightly.

Again and again, thank you!

INDEX

Quotations are reprinted from:

Shanti Christo Foundation, *The Way of Mastery*, Shanti Christo Foundation, 2004

New King James Version, *The Holy Bible*, Thomas Nelson, 1982

Thomas Verny, M.D., with John Kelly, *The Secret Life of the Unborn Child*, Dell, 1982

Baba Adegun Iwindara Reece, *ObaKaye Temple Field Manual: Finding Your Way with the Orisa*, 2018

Malidoma Patrice Some, *The Healing Wisdom of Africa*, TarcherPerigee, 1999

Hermes Trismegistus, *The Emerald Tablet*

Barbara Breenan, *Hands of Light*, Bantam Books, 1988

James Baldwin, *The Fire Next Time*, The Dial Press, 1963

Iyanla Vanzant, *21 Days of Forgiveness*, Smiley Books, 2017

bell hooks, *all about love*, HarperCollins, 2001

Sobonfu Some, *The Spirit of Intimacy*, William Morrow, 2000

William Bascom, *Ifa Divination: Communication Between Gods and Men in West Africa*, Indiana University Press, 1991

Awo Fa'lokun Fatunmbi, *Ori: The Ifa Concept of Consciousness*, 2014

Don Miquel Ruiz, *The Four Agreements*, Amber-Allen Publishing, 1997